> *"We make sense of the world through mental models, not just accumulating facts. Mental models help us recognize patterns. A good model allows us to see different things every time we look at it! The best mental models are simple, flexible, and open enough to capture complex situations and encourage us to see more, and ask better questions."*

- Marc Applebaum, PhD

Many of the designations used by manufacturers and sellers to distinguish their products are claimed as trademarks. Where these designations appear in this book and the authors were aware of a trademark claim, the designations have been printed in initial caps, all caps, or with appropriate registration symbols.

The authors have taken care in the preparation of this document, but make no expressed or implied warranty of any kind and assume no responsibility for errors or omissions. No liability is assumed for incidental or consequential damages in connection with or arising out of the use of the information contained herein.

'Get To Done' is a registered Trademark of Get To Done, LLC

'Scrum Dictionary' is a registered Trademark of ScrumZone.org, which is an organization focused on Organizational Scrum: Single-Team and Multi-Team.

Book Design by Tuna Traffic, LLC.

This Scrum Guidebook ©2019, 3Back LLC, except for "The (Annotated) Scrum Guide" which is copyrighted as follows:
 - Scrum Guide ©2017 Scrum.Org and ScrumInc
 - Annotations ©2018, 2019 3Back LLC

All Copyrights are offered for license under the Attribution Share-Alike license of Creative Commons, accessible at http://creativecommons.org/licenses/by-sa/4.0/legalcode and also described in summary form at http://creativecommons.org/licenses/by-sa/4.0/. By utilizing this Scrum Guidebook you acknowledge and agree that you have read and agree to be bound by the terms of the Attribution Share-Alike license of Creative Commons.

First Edition publication date: January 15, 2019
7th Version publication date: September 6, 2019

ISBN-13: 9781794186989

SCRUM
GUIDEBOOK

ANALYSIS OF THE 2017 SCRUM GUIDE

Dan Rawsthorne, PhD, CST
Chief Scientist, 3Back LLC
ScrumZone.org

Doug Shimp, CST
President, 3Back LLC
ScrumZone.org

The (Annotated) Scrum Guide

Scrum Dictionary

Nine Zones of Scrum

The Agile Manifesto

Intro to STS and MTS (Scaling)

Contents of Guidebook

Analysis of the 2017 Scrum Guide

Dan Rawsthorne, PhD, CST, and Doug Shimp, CST
3Back LLC, ScrumZone.org

Table of Contents

Purpose of Analysis

In practice, Scrum is a vague concept. There are many different, incompatible, kinds of Scrum; and for each of these kinds of Scrum, there can be different descriptions. We like the Scrum that is described in the 2017 Scrum Guide, but we find the description to be lacking. We wrote the *Scrum Handbooks* (both *STS* and *MTS*) in order to provide a different description of Scrum, that was true to the Scrum of the Scrum Guide, but whose description is more useful for Organizations trying to use Scrum.

So, in order to verify that we 'got the Scrum right,' we analyzed the 2017 Scrum Guide, and made an annotated version of it for people to review. There are over 60 annotations, and each contains one or more observations made about what we find in the Scrum Guide. Throughout this analysis, you will see references to these Annotations, which are found in *"The (Annotated) Scrum Guide,"* which is included in its entirety in the second section of this book.

The Scrum Guide Simplifies the Problem

The 2017 Scrum Guide provides a description of Scrum tailored to the following situation:

- A single Scrum Team delivering a single Product to a single group of Stakeholders; where
- Each Sprint is treated as a 'Small Project' that has an anticipated result.

As our experience (and the Scrum Guide itself) shows, this is not the *only* situation that Scrum pertains to. The following sub-sections of this analysis address the Scrum Guide's treatment of these two issues.

There are Two Definitions of Product

There are two types of Products defined in the Scrum Guide. The first type is the one we usually think of: a Product is something we build and deliver to customers and users. These Products are deliverables that have Stakeholders, require-ments, users, schedules, budgets, and so on... they are exactly what we think they should be. For the sake of this analysis, I will call these products "Product-Products", because they are the Products we normally think of as Products.

But, because Scrum is about Teams, and the Scrum Guide is about Scrum, the Scrum Guide defines another type of Product – one that is Team-focused. This product consists of "the deliverables that result from the Development Team's work" (see Annotation 11), and we will refer to this as a "Team-Product", since each Dev Team (and each Scrum Team) produces exactly one of them.

Now, the relationship between Product-Products and Team-Products is straightforward:

- More than one Team's Team-Product can contribute deliverables to a single Product-Product, or
- A single Team-Product can contribute deliverables to more than one Product-Product.

In general, there is a many-to-many relationship between Team-Products and Product-Products (see Figure 1). Except for a short paragraph about two Teams working on the same Product (Annotation 51), the Scrum guide is *completely silent* about this issue. That does *not* mean there is no issue...

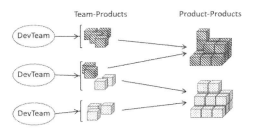

Figure 1: The Relationship between Team-Products and Product-Products

The Scrum Guide says that *every* Product has a Product Backlog, which is "an ordered list of everything that is known to be needed in the product" and a single Product Owner, who is "responsible for the Product Backlog, including its content, availability, and ordering" (Annotation 49). For Product-Products, this is all the Scrum Guide says. For Team-Products, however, the Scrum Guide is more explicit:

- The Team-Product Owner is the Scrum Team Member who is accountable for the Development Team getting their Work to "Done" (including technical Quality), and maximizing the value of that work – whether it produces Team-Product or not. (Annotations 11 and 14). The Team-Product Owner is not just about the Team-Product and its technical Quality, but also about *all* the work the Development Team does...

- Even further, the Team-Product Backlog is expanded to include *all* the work the Scrum Team is doing, whether or not the work is creating Team-Product (Annotation 15). So, the Team-Product Backlog should, more appropriately, be called the 'Team Work Backlog', which includes *all* the work the Scrum Team does, including non-deliverable work done by the Development Team (Spikes, Analysis, internal Training, etc.), the Scrum Master, and the Product Owner.

Figure 2 shows a complete picture of the relationships between different kinds of Products, Product Backlogs, and Product Owners.

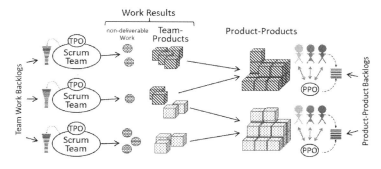

Figure 2: The Complete picture of Products, Product Backlogs, and Product Owners

In this diagram we see a 'funny' notation for the Team Work Backlogs. The funnel shape, curved arrow, and different shading indicate that Refinement is taking place (see Annotation 52) that (possibly) includes the creation, or identification, of non-deliverable work.

The Scrum Guide strives hard to be simple and under-standable, and it clearly wants to ignore the complexity inherent in the decomposition and flow of work items between the (possibly many) Product-Product Backlogs to the (possibly many) Team Work Backlogs. Therefore, the *Scrum Guide* simplifies the vast majority of its discussion to the case where:

- There is a single Scrum Team developing a single Product,
- The same person plays both the Team-Product Owner and Product-Product Owner roles, and
- The Team Work Backlog and the Product-Product Backlog are collapsed to a single Backlog, which is referred to as the Product Backlog.

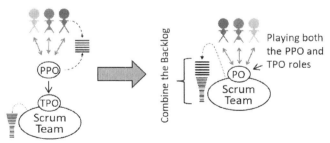

Figure 3: The Simplification the Scrum Guide Makes

In other words, the 2017 Scrum Guide presents the situation we see in Figure 2, but only provides a description of Scrum for the simple case seen in Figure 3. The only exception to this is a single paragraph that references multiple Teams working on the same Product (Annotation 51), which says: "Multiple Scrum Teams often work together on the same product. One Product Backlog is used to describe the upcoming work on the product. A Product Backlog attribute that groups items may then be employed."

In general, this is a scaling problem that looks like the 'left side' of Figure 4, but if we assume that the same person is playing all the Product Owner roles in this situation, and we collapse all the Backlogs to a single Backlog, it looks like the right side of Figure 4. We believe that this is the intent of this paragraph of the Scrum Guide.

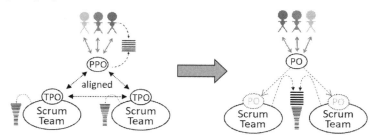

Figure 4: The Simplest Scaling Solution

To be precise, the specific problem on the left side of Figure 4 is solved if 1) the same person plays all three Product Owner Roles, 2) there is a single Product Backlog (which both Teams refine), and 3) there is a grouping attribute that allows each Team to know which Items 'belong' to them. This is what we see on the right side of Figure 4, and, therefore, solves this specific problem.

However, this does not solve the general problem that is 'hinted at' by the left side of Figure 4. In particular, the same person cannot play *all* the PO roles if there are *many* Scrum Teams involved (some people believe that there is an upper bound of eight Teams, we believe the number is smaller). Clearly, the biggest problem in this small scaling situation is keeping all the 'involved' Product Owners in alignment about what needs to be done, and this alignment is one of the problems *all* scaling methods address.

Scrum Guide uses the 'Small Project' Strategy

The 2017 Scrum Guide assumes a development strategy where each Sprint is a 'Small Project' (see Annotation 30). Not only is there a single Scrum Team, and a single Product, but that Product is developed Sprint-to-Sprint, with the Scrum Team forecasting the anticipated Increment to be produced each Sprint (see Annotations 36 and 37). The whole Scrum Guide describes Scrum from this Point of View.

This is not the only point of view to have; we don't even think it's the most common. In our experience, most Scrum Teams are doing 'Continuous Development', where the Backlog represents a Continuous Flow of work for the Team, and the Sprint simply defines the duration until reviewing the "Done" Results.

At the beginning of the Scrum Guide, it says that Scrum has been used to "release products and enhancements, as frequently as many times per day." This is clearly true, as we've all seen it. In many 'Continuous Development' environments, these 'enhancements' are 'bugs' that come flying at the Team in a random, chaotic, fashion – from many different directions – and a typical objective for the Team during a Sprint is something like *"fix all the show-stopper bugs that come in and then do whatever other work you have time for."* The Team-Product Owner is on the Scrum Team, "Optimizing the value of the work the Development Team performs," and is often the one who determines (on the fly) which bugs to fix and whatever other work to do. In this case, it is difficult to forecast anything at all; and it is unlikely that there is a specific "anticipated increment" to be produced.

In fact, we'll go even further. We believe that Scrum Teams are *always* doing 'Continuous Development', but sometimes there *is* an "anticipated increment" to be produced at the end of the Sprint. In other words, sometimes a Sprint *is* like a 'Small Project' – even while doing 'Continuous Development. In this case, if there is actually an "anticipated increment" to be produced, there is likely to be complicated Sprint Planning – as is described in the Scrum Guide. In general, though, we believe that Sprint Planning can be a *lot* simpler...

Other Important Results of the Analysis

In our experience, many people have misunderstood what is said in (or implied by) the 2017 Scrum Guide. In the following sections we describe some of the additional conclusions we found through analysis of the Scrum Guide.

The Need for a Business Owner

In the case where there are multiple Product Owners (both TPOs and PPOs), they must stay in alignment about what will be worked on, and who (which Team) will do it. In our opinion, this is a 'People thing', not a 'Process thing'; as we believe in the Agile Manifesto ("we have come to value Individuals and interactions over processes and tools," remember...).

This could be complicated if there are many Product Owners involved, so let's simplify this discussion to the case where the Product Owners are involved in a flow like we see in Figures Figure 2 and Figure 4. We believe that the Product Owners involved (both TPOs and PPOs) need to discuss the problem of who does what, and figure it out amongst themselves – this is what supplies the 'alignment' they need. Since we're being agile, this may need to be done often, if not 'all the time'.

Since these Product Owners may not come to agreement (get aligned) by themselves, they probably need their own Product Owner to 'break the deadlock' and own the decision. So, we recommend putting all these Product Owners on their own Scrum Team, and give them their own Product Owner, who we call the Business Owner (BO).

We call this role a Business Owner because their job is to maximize the value for the Business, not look out for a particular Team (which is the TPO's job) or a particular Product (which is the PPO's job). We (at 3Back) call this Team a "Flow Mgmt Team", as it manages the flow of work from the Stake-holders to the Scrum Teams – and the Business Owner (this Teams TPO) is the 'owner' of the flow…

The Flow Mgmt Team is a part of the SSwS (Scaling Scrum with Scrum®) framework. SSwS is the only scrum-based scaling method/framework that allows scaling with multiple Product-Products (as well as multiple Teams), as far as we know[1].

In Annotation 13 we see that there is likely to be a Business Owner providing GOs (Guidance and Objectives) for their

---

[1] Scrum.org has "the Nexus" and Scrum@Scale has the "Product Owner Team", but they both restrict the scaling to a single Product-Product. SAFe allows for multiple Product-Products – if you look at it just right – but it is not actually Scrum-based.

Organization (collection of Teams). In particular, Business Owners provide GOs to their subordinate Product Owners (both TPOs and PPOs), who will refer to these GOs as they make decisions about their Backlogs (both Team-Product and Product-Product).

Better Understanding of the Sprint Goal

Because of the 'Small Project' strategy that is endemic in the Scrum Guide, many of the descriptions of the Sprint Goal in the Scrum Guide have something to do with the forecasted or anticipated increment (see Annotations 31, 33, and 35). This is clearly inappropriate for most Teams engaged in 'continuous development'... Ultimately, though, the Scrum Guide coughs up the correct definition (Annotation 38) when it says (our paraphrasing):

> The Sprint Goal is something that the Scrum Team members agree to accomplish *together* within the Sprint. The Sprint Goal defines success for the Sprint, and the Team will do *whatever it takes* to meet it. Committing to the Sprint Goal, rather than the Sprint Backlog, allows the Team the 'wiggle room' needed to avoid compromising Quality while it works.

We think this is a great definition, and it is supported by the Scrum Guide.

Better Understanding of What "Done" is

Many people have defined the Definition of "Done" (DoD) to be the Quality constraints a Team uses when it creates Product. This is not completely true. While the Quality constraints are part of "Done" (see Annotation 63), the definition of "Done" is actually (our paraphrasing):

"… the shared, common, understanding, between the Team and Stakeholders, of what it means for a Product Backlog Item or Increment to be complete."

In other words, each Backlog Item has its own definition of "Done", as well as the Increment, and this "Done" is not limited to Quality criteria (e.g. it could include functional Acceptance Criteria). We can also conclude that once a "not Done" Item is included in an Increment, the Increment can never be "Done" until that Item gets to "Done" (see Annotation 60). We believe this last conclusion is important, and is an example of the aphorism 'one bad apple spoils the barrel.'

The Scrum Master Finally has some Authority

There has long been a tension between the Team's Scrum Master and the Team-Product Owner. On the one hand, we know that the Team's Scrum Master is accountable for the Team's Scrum Mastering (see Annotation 46). On the other hand, the Team-Product Owner is accountable for the content and the ordering of the Team-Product Backlog (Team Work Backlog), which includes the Scrum Mastering work the Scrum Team does (Annotation 15).

This creates a potential collision of accountabilities, since the Team-Product Owner may decide not to prioritize what the Team's Scrum Master wants or needs. This problem has been somewhat mitigated in the 2017 Scrum Guide because the Team's Sprint Backlog is required to have (at least) one improvement Story in it (see Annotation 54). This Story is often called a Kaizen, and guarantees that *at least one* Scrum Mastering 'thing' will be done in each Sprint.

Conclusion

The 2017 Scrum Guide describes a version of Scrum that is balanced and uncomplicated. Unfortunately, the description is incomplete, as it only describes the case of a single Scrum Team, delivering a single Product, using a development strategy that treats each Sprint as a 'Small Project'.

This incomplete description has caused misunderstandings about what Scrum is, and the purpose of this analysis is to help clear up some of them.

The biggest, and most important, misunderstanding about Scrum is about Product Ownership. Many people believe that the Scrum Guide says that there *can only be* a single Product with accompanying Product Backlog and Product Owner.

In fact, the Scrum Guide describes two types of Products, each with its own type of Product Backlog and Product Owner. In the general case, which has many Teams delivering many different Products, the complete picture is as shown in Figure 2, and I recommend you go look at that section again.

Because all Teams' Product Owners are accountable for the value of their Scrum Team's work, they are accountable for the Quality of the work, as well. They are accountable for meeting the Sprint Goal; they are accountable for the Quality of the Work; they are accountable to make the flow a 'Pull not Push'; they are accountable for pushing back against unreasonable demands; they are accountable for *everything* that may affect the value of the work getting to "Done".

The second big misunderstanding about Scrum is that development with Scrum *must use* the 'Small Project' method of development, which requires heavy-duty Sprint Planning that produces a forecasted, anticipated, Product Increment. In fact, most Scrum Teams do 'continuous development', which does not require a forecast (but there could be one) and, since there is no forecast, they can use light-weight forms of Sprint Planning.

There are several other (smaller) results of our analysis involving misunderstandings of Business Ownership, the Sprint Goal, what "Done" means, and the purpose of a Sprintly Kaizen.

We developed the *Scrum Handbooks* to expand the description of Scrum beyond this simple version contained in the 2017 Scrum Guide. Without going into any detail, we see a continuum:

1. The 2017 Scrum Guide describes Scrum in the case of a single Scrum Team delivering a single Product using the 'Small Project' strategy;
2. The *Scrum Handbook: Single-Team Scrum (STS)* expands to describe a single Scrum Team delivering (possibly many) Products while doing 'Continuous Development' (which includes the 'Small Project' strategy); and
3. The *Scrum Handbook: Multi-Team Scrum (MTS)* expands even further to describe multiple Scrum Teams delivering (possibly many) Products while doing 'Continuous Development'.

In all three cases, the underlying Scrum is the same, with the exception that the *Handbooks* bring back the Abnormal Termination, which the Scrum Guide inexplicably removed. In other words, with this single exception, these are three different descriptions of the *same* Scrum, but in different contexts.

I hope that this analysis helps you with your Scrum. Happy Scrumming!

Annotated

The Scrum Guide

The Definitive Guide to Scrum: The Rules of the Game

November 2017

Developed and sustained by Ken Schwaber and Jeff Sutherland

Annotations by Dan Rawsthorne and Doug Shimp

Table of Contents

16

Purpose of the Scrum Guide

Scrum is a framework for developing, delivering, and sustaining complex products. This Guide contains the definition of Scrum. This definition consists of Scrum's roles, events, artifacts, and the rules that bind them together. Ken Schwaber and Jeff Sutherland developed Scrum; the Scrum Guide is written and provided by them. Together, they stand behind the Scrum Guide.

Annotation 1: Annotations Description...

The Scrum Guide is a description (or model) of Scrum that is accepted by Scrum.org, the Scrum Alliance, and others, as the standard description of Scrum. The purpose of these annotations is to analyze the 2017 Scrum Guide, as it is written, and compare it to other descriptions of Scrum, previous Scrum Guides, and the like. The annotations we add to this Scrum guide are our attempt to dig in, and explore,

> what the Guide is trying to tell us... All the annotations will be found in gray boxes like this one... Our goal is to analyze, and comment on, what we see in the Scrum Guide.

Definition of Scrum

Scrum (n): A framework within which people can address complex adaptive problems, while productively and creatively delivering products of the highest possible value. Scrum is:

- Lightweight
- Simple to understand
- Difficult to master

Scrum is a process framework that has been used to manage work on complex products since the early 1990s. Scrum is not a process, technique, or definitive method. Rather, it is a framework within which you can employ various processes and techniques. Scrum makes clear the relative efficacy of your product management and work techniques so that you can continuously improve the product, the team, and the working environment.

The Scrum framework consists of Scrum Teams and their associated roles, events, artifacts, and rules. Each component within the framework serves a specific purpose and is essential to Scrum's success and usage.

The rules of Scrum bind together the roles, events, and artifacts, governing the relationships and interaction between them. The rules of Scrum are described throughout the body of this document.

Specific tactics for using the Scrum framework vary and are described elsewhere.

> Annotation 2: Scrum is not prescriptive...
>
> This is an important section, as it points out that the guidance in the Scrum Guide is **not** prescriptive in how to use Scrum. From the title we see that the Scrum Guide considers itself "The Definitive Guide to Scrum: The Rules of the Game", and here it says that how we use the rules in our environment is up to us.
>
> In other words, the Scrum Guide's description of Scrum is a model (or framework) that provides guidance for us to use when instantiating Scrum within our Organizations. Scrum, as defined in the Scrum Guide, is **not** a comprehensive recipe for success – it consists of guidance, advice, and patterns that can form the basis for addressing complex problems.
>
> The phrases "complex adaptive problems" and "complex products" are undefined, and it is left to the reader to determine what they mean. We have seen Scrum used to develop products of varying levels of complexity, from the simple to the complicated to the almost incomprehensible; so readers are invited to determine, for themselves, if understanding these phrases is important to fully understand this Scrum Guide.

Uses of Scrum

Scrum was initially developed for managing and developing products. Starting in the early 1990s, Scrum has been used extensively, worldwide, to:

1. Research and identify viable markets, technologies, and product capabilities;

2. Develop products and enhancements;
3. Release products and enhancements, as frequently as many times per day;
4. Develop and sustain Cloud (online, secure, on-demand) and other operational environments for product use; and,
5. Sustain and renew products.

Scrum has been used to develop software, hardware, embedded software, networks of interacting function, autonomous vehicles, schools, government, marketing, managing the operation of organizations and almost everything we use in our daily lives, as individuals and societies.

As technology, market, and environmental complexities and their interactions have rapidly increased, Scrum's utility in dealing with complexity is proven daily.

Scrum proved especially effective in iterative and incremental knowledge transfer. Scrum is now widely used for products, services, and the management of the parent organization.

The essence of Scrum is a small team of people. The individual team is highly flexible and adaptive. These strengths continue operating in single, several, many, and networks of teams that develop, release, operate and sustain the work and work products of thousands of people. They collaborate and interoperate through sophisticated development architectures and target release environments.

When the words "develop" and "development" are used in the Scrum Guide, they refer to complex work, such as those types identified above.

> Annotation 3: "Product" means "Results"...
>
> What I take from this section is that the word "Product" is

misleading, and restrictive, when talking about Scrum. This section basically says that Scrum allows/helps a small team of people to produce Results for Stakeholders, and that these Results can take many forms. In the same way that "develop" and "development" refer to any (potentially) complex work, the word "Product" simply refers to the (appropriate) Results produced by the Team or delivered by the Organization.

Scrum Theory

Scrum is founded on empirical process control theory, or empiricism. Empiricism asserts that knowledge comes from experience and making decisions based on what is known. Scrum employs an iterative, incremental approach to optimize predictability and control risk.

Three pillars uphold every implementation of empirical process control: transparency, inspection, and adaptation.

Transparency

Significant aspects of the process must be visible to those responsible for the outcome. Transparency requires those aspects be defined by a common standard so observers share a common understanding of what is being seen.

For example:

- A common language referring to the process must be shared by all participants; and,
- Those performing the work and those inspecting the resulting increment must share a common definition of "Done".

> ### Annotation 4: A common understanding of "Done"
>
> Transparency requires a common understanding, between those doing the work and those reviewing and/or inspecting the work, of what it means to be "Done." This is important, and the concept of "Done" will be explored in depth in the Annotations.

Inspection

Scrum users must frequently inspect Scrum artifacts and progress toward a Sprint Goal to detect undesirable variances. Their inspection should not be so frequent that inspection gets in the way of the work. Inspections are most beneficial when diligently performed by skilled inspectors at the point of work.

> ### Annotation 5: Inspection not about variances...
>
> In this context, inspection is done in order to determine if Adaptation is needed. The first sentence of this paragraph is both too specific and incorrect: inspections are not limited to detecting variances from a target and, even it were, the "Sprint Goal" (which is a specific thing that will be defined and discussed later) is not that target. We believe that a better first sentence is "Scrum Users must frequently inspect artifacts, processes, and progress." and then start the second sentence with "These inspections..."

Adaptation

If an inspector determines that one or more aspects of a process deviate outside acceptable limits, and that the resulting product will be unacceptable, the process or the material being processed must be adjusted. An adjustment must be made as soon as possible to minimize further deviation.

> **Annotation 6: "and" should be "and/or"...**
>
> This is just a typo. The second clause of the first sentence should start with "and/or", not just "and".

Scrum prescribes four formal events for inspection and adaptation, as described in the Scrum Events section of this document:

- Sprint Planning
- Daily Scrum
- Sprint Review
- Sprint Retrospective

> **Annotation 7: Events are about feedback and discussion...**
>
> Each of these 'inspect and adapt' events is about feedback and discussion. The inspectors' job is to provide feedback to, and have discussions with, the Scrum Team so that they can adapt. Depending on the event, the inspectors can be external Stakeholders or members of the Scrum Team itself.

Scrum Values

When the values of commitment, courage, focus, openness and respect are embodied and lived by the Scrum Team, the Scrum pillars of transparency, inspection, and adaptation come to life and build trust for everyone. The Scrum Team members learn and explore those values as they work with the Scrum roles, events, and artifacts.

Successful use of Scrum depends on people becoming more proficient in living these five values. People personally commit to achieving the goals of the Scrum Team. The Scrum Team members have courage to do the right thing and work on tough problems. Everyone focuses on the work of the Sprint and the goals of the Scrum Team. The Scrum Team and its stakeholders agree to be open about all the work and the challenges with performing the work. Scrum Team members respect each other to be capable, independent people.

> **Annotation 8: Mission, vision, goal, objective are all synonyms**
>
> This is a great section, as it stresses the importance of value-driven people. However, there is also reference to the "goals of the Scrum Team." The word "goal" is used throughout the Scrum Guide, culminating with the definition of a Scrum artifact called the "Sprint Goal". Don't be confused. Except for the phrase "Sprint Goal", the words vision, mission, goal, and objective are loosely used as synonyms throughout this document... and have no specific meanings within the model. You should treat them as 'syntactical sugar' and try to maintain focus on the Scrum Model as a whole.

The Scrum Team

The Scrum Team consists of a Product Owner, the Development Team, and a Scrum Master. Scrum Teams are self-organizing and cross-functional. Self-organizing teams choose how best to accomplish their work, rather than being directed by others outside the team. Cross-functional teams have all competencies needed to accomplish the work without depending on others not part of the team. The team model in

Scrum is designed to optimize flexibility, creativity, and productivity. The Scrum Team has proven itself to be increasingly effective for all the earlier stated uses, and any complex work.

Annotation 9: PO and SM are members of the self-organized Scrum Team...

This is an amazing paragraph; it is filled with good stuff.

1) <u>SM and PO part of self-organized Team</u>. Every Scrum Team has both a Product Owner and a Scrum Master – and that it is the whole Scrum Team that is self-organized. In many (if not most) early descriptions of Scrum the Product Owner and Scrum Master are **not** described as members of the self-organized Team – the self-organization is limited to the Development Team. This is actually a big deal, as you can't just *say* somebody is on a self-organized Team without them actually *being* on the Team – the fact that the Team is self-organized makes that impossible. In other words, the Team's Product Owner and Scrum Master are just-as-much Team Members as everybody else; it's not just 'lip service' to say that they are on the Team.

2) <u>Everybody shares the work</u>. Because the Scrum Team contains both a Product Owner and a Scrum Master (as well as a Development Team), the Scrum Team does Development, Product Ownership, and Scrum Mastering. Since the Scrum Team is self-organized, the Scrum Team determines how to do each of these things – the Scrum Team is responsible for all of it. In other words, if the Scrum Team decides to do so, it is 'perfectly legal' for its Product Owner and Scrum Master to do development work, and it is 'perfectly legal' for any team member to help with Product Ownership and Scrum

---

Mastering. This potential sharing of the work is an intrinsic part of Scrum, and not something that can be removed from the Scrum Team; not by management, not by process, not by anybody...

3) <u>Roles or People</u>? The Product Owner and Scrum Master are often thought of as roles, not people. However, we promised that out Annotations would 'call them as we see them', and the Scrum Guide is quite insistent on calling the Team's Product Owner a 'person' – so I will assume that they are both people and not roles. In any case, though, the whole Team can share in doing the Product Ownership and Scrum Mastering, as we discussed in 2), above.

4) <u>The Scrum Team is self-contained (cross-functional)</u>. In this paragraph the Scrum Guide defines a "cross-functional team" to mean it has "all competencies needed to accomplish the work without depending on others not part of the team." (Note: We prefer to call this a "self-contained team" because it's a more intention-revealing name.) Since there is Product Ownership and Scrum Mastering on the Scrum Team (see 2), above), this means that the Team can, within itself, do all the PM and SM work – as well an any Development work – itself. And, this means getting that work all the way to "Done", including the Quality constraints.

5) <u>A simple misperception</u>. The final sentence in the previous paragraph seems to imply that *every* Scrum Team is effective and delivering. I don't think that could possibly be what is intended, so I think the final sentence is actually trying to say: "Scrum Teams have proven themselves to be..." which does not imply the 'every'...

Scrum Teams deliver products iteratively and incrementally, maximizing opportunities for feedback. Incremental deliveries of "Done" product ensure a potentially useful version of working product is always available.

> **Annotation 10: Scrum Teams provide Deliverable Results...**
>
> There are two important things in this paragraph:
>
> 1. that products are deliverables, not just things to be developed, and
>
> 2. that Scrum Teams, not Development Teams, deliver the products.
>
> Since we already know (see Annotation 3) that products are simple Results, we can say that products are the Deliverable Results of Scrum Teams, which are produced by their Development Teams.

The Product Owner

The Product Owner is responsible for maximizing the value of the product resulting from work of the Development Team. How this is done may vary widely across organizations, Scrum Teams, and individuals.

> **Annotation 11: The Scrum Team has its own Product, Backlog, and Product Owner**
>
> This paragraph is very important, and clarifies one of the main differentiators of 'Scrum Guide Scrum' and many other Scrum descriptions. We already know that there is a (physical or virtual) Product Owner on the Scrum Team (Annotation 9), and this paragraph clarifies that the product

the Team's Product Owner 'owns' is "the product resulting from work of the Development Team." And, since a product consists of Deliverable Results (Annotation 10), we can make a definition:

> "the Team's Product consists of the Deliverable Results produced by the Development Team's work,"

and we will call this product the **Team-Product** as we continue analyzing the Scrum Guide. This definition clarifies what product the Product Owner is responsible for.

We are sure this wording is not accidental. As we'll see later (Annotation 49), each product has a product backlog, which is "an ordered list of everything that is known to be needed in the product," so this Team-Product must have a Product Backlog, which (like the Product) will be specific to this Scrum Team. In our analysis we will refer to this Backlog as the 'Team-Product Backlog' and refer to the Team's Product Owner as the 'Team-Product Owner'.

Why is this important? Because, later in this Guide, we will see another definition of Product Owner, based on another definition of 'product' – and we'll need to be able to tell them apart. The confusion is understandable, as we'll discuss later.

So, let me summarize so far. We know:

- Every Scrum Team has its own Team-Product, the Scrum Team's Deliverable Results produced by the Development Team's work;

- Every Scrum Team has its own Team-Product Backlog, an ordered list of everything that is known to be needed in these deliverables (the Team-Product); and

> • Every Scrum Team has its own Team-Product Owner, who is the Team Member who is responsible for maximizing the value of these deliverables.

The Product Owner is the sole person responsible for managing the Product Backlog. Product Backlog management includes:

> **Annotation 12: The Team-Product Owner manages the Team-Product Backlog**
>
> Just noting that it is explicit that the Team-Product Owner manages the Team-Product Backlog.

- Clearly expressing Product Backlog items;
- Ordering the items in the Product Backlog to best achieve goals and missions;

> **Annotation 13: We need a Business Owner**
>
> This clause raises an important question: 'where do the goals and missions come from?' Clearly, they come from somewhere within either the Stakeholder Community or the Team's Organization, and they may be 'owned' by some role within the Organization. The one thing we know for sure is that the Scrum Guide does **not** require that these goals and missions originate from the Team-Product Owner. They are clearly important for the Scrum Team, but the Scrum Guide does not tell us how or where they come from.
>
> Since we like to have tidy models, with as few loose ends as possible, we posit the existence of another role, the **Business Owner**, who will be the source/owner for the Goals and Missions for the Organization. We believe that this role (or something like it) is implied here, since the Goals and

> Missions must come from somewhere, and should be 'owned' by someone.
>
> In order to further tidy up the model, we assume that the Business Owner also serves as the person who the Team-Product Owner is accountable to (see Annotation 16). The Business Owner role is not *defined* in the Scrum Guide, but I believe that it, or something like it, is *implied* by the Scrum Guide...

- Optimizing the value of the work the Development Team performs;

> Annotation 14: Team-Product Owner maximizes the value of *all* the DevTeam's work
>
> Note the clarification that the Team-Product Owner is not just maximizing the value of the product (Deliverable Results) produced by the Development Team's work, but optimizing the value of *all* the work the Development Team does. Value has a more specific meaning for product than non-product, because value for product-related work is realized when the work gets to "Done" (Annotation 20). We also know that "Done" includes appropriate technical Quality (Annotation 60), so this means that the Team's Product Owner is responsible for making sure that product (deliverable work) gets to "Done", with appropriate technical Quality.
>
> In other words, we can define the Team-Product Owner as:
>
> > "The Team-Product Owner is the Scrum Team Member who is responsible for maximizing the value of the Development Team's Work, whether the work produces Deliverable Results or not. Further, the Team-

> Product Owner is responsible for assuring that all Deliverable Results get to "Done", including Technical Quality."
>
> This is a statement we can get behind. It is simple, straightforward, and useful.

- Ensuring that the Product Backlog is visible, transparent, and clear to all, and shows what the Scrum Team will work on next; and,

---

Annotation 15: The Team-Product Backlog is actually the Team's Work Backlog...

This paragraph expands the definition of the Team-Product Backlog, as well.

- So far (Annotation 11), we know that the Team-Product Backlog is an ordered list of everything that is known to be needed in the Deliverable Results produced by the Development Team's work; and

- Now we learn that the Team-Product Backlog includes *all* the work the Scrum Team will work on next.

These are not the same thing. There is non-deliverable work, there is Product-Ownership work (analysis, discovery, strategy, etc.), there is Scrum Mastering work (removing impediments, process coaching, etc.), and all of this work is now included in the Team-Product Backlog. Basically, there are two different kinds of work: work that produces Deliverable Results, and work that doesn't. Different Teams and Organizations deal with this distinction in different ways; all we know is that it must be dealt with. In any case, we can see that the Team-Product Backlog should, more appropriately, be called the Team Work Backlog.

There is also a trap in this paragraph. The phrase "clear to all" could cause some to over-specify and/or prematurely-specify the Team-Product Backlog Items. Either of these problems can lead to Big Design Up Front (BDUF), which is the antithesis of agility. The trick is to have the Team Work Backlog (Team-Product Backlog) contain 'just enough' information to control the flow of work through the Scrum Team.

- Ensuring the Development Team understands items in the Product Backlog to the level needed.

The Product Owner may do the above work, or have the Development Team do it. However, the Product Owner remains accountable.

Annotation 16: Team-Product Owner accountable for *almost all of* the Team's Work

This paragraph says two things:

- By saying "[t]he Product Owner may do the above work, or have the Development Team do it," this is restating that the Scrum Team is self-organized; and

- It changes the word 'responsible' (which is seen earlier) to 'accountable', which is a pretty strong (and correct, in our view) word.

For those of you that have confusion over "responsible" versus "accountable", here are short definitions that are appropriate in this context (that of a person being accountable):

- Accountable – required or expected to explain/justify actions or decisions;
- Responsible – having an obligation to do something.

In other words, Accountability focuses on ownership and Responsibility focuses on doing work. In this case, the Scrum and Development Teams are responsible for doing Work, while the Team-Product Owner is accountable to people outside the Scrum Team (perhaps the Business Owner) for the Work being done.

There is still one ambiguous point. We know that the Team-Product Backlog (Team Work Backlog) contains the work for the complete Scrum Team, and we know that the Team-Product Owner is accountable for the value of the work of the Development Team. We think it's safe to say that the Team-Product Owner is also accountable for the Scrum Team's Product Ownership work. But, is the Team-Product Owner accountable for the Team's Scrum Mastering work?

No. The Team's Scrum Master is accountable for the Team's Scrum Mastering work. I know that, thus far, there is no evidence of this in the Scrum Guide. It doesn't say so in the section on the Scrum Master, either. However... Later (Annotation 46), in the **"Sprint Retrospective"** section, there is an offhand comment that says: "The Scrum Master participates as a peer team member in the meeting from the accountability over the Scrum process." It just pops up out of nowhere, but it clears up the question of who is accountable for Scrum Mastering...

The Product Owner is one person, not a committee. The Product Owner may represent the desires of a committee in the Product Backlog, but those wanting to change a Product Backlog item's priority must address the Product Owner.

> **Annotation 17: There is only one Team-Product Owner...**
>
> This statement is in the **"Scrum Team"** section of the Scrum Guide, and it simply means that there is only one Scrum Team Member playing the Team-Product Owner role. There may be others, outside the Team, that are involved in Product Ownership (as we'll discuss later), but none of them is the Team-Product Owner.

For the Product Owner to succeed, the entire organization must respect his or her decisions. The Product Owner's decisions are visible in the content and ordering of the Product Backlog. No one can force the Development Team to work from a different set of requirements.

> **Annotation 18: Team-Product Owner's decisions must be respected**
>
> This is the most important statement about the Team-Product Owner in the Scrum Guide. This sentence, or one very much like it, appears in every description of Scrum written by Ken Schwaber. Personally, we like the slightly stronger version of this statement that is found in the 2016 Scrum Guide, which we repeat here with appropriate changes to emphasize which Team is involved and to clarify that the Team-Product Backlog is actually the Scrum Team Work Backlog:
>
> "For the Team-Product Owner to succeed, the entire

> organization must respect his or her decisions. The Team-Product Owner's decisions are visible in the content and ordering of the Team-Product Backlog (Team Work Backlog). No one is allowed to tell the Development Team to work from a different set of requirements, and the Development Team isn't allowed to act on what anyone else says."

Why did this statement change? Is it possible that the 2017 Scrum Guide is saying that the Development Team *is allowed* to work on a different set of requirements if they do it voluntarily? We can't believe that's true, and simply think that the 2017 wording is flawed.

In any case, we love this statement (as it is intended to be), as it clearly points out that the Development Team needs to be protected from everybody outside the Scrum Team, even if they are in other Ownership roles. We believe this protection should be supplied by the Business Owner (because the Team belongs to the Business), the Team-Product Owner (in order to maintain ownership), and the Team's Scrum Master (as an impediment-removal thing).

But, this paragraph also creates a conundrum. On the one hand, it says that the Team-Product Owner decides on the content and the ordering of the Team-Product Backlog (Team Work Backlog); and we know that includes the Scrum Mastering work the Scrum Team does (Annotation 15). On the other hand, we will learn that the Team's Scrum Master is accountable for the Team's Scrum Mastering work (Annotation 46). This creates a potential collision of accountabilities, since the Team-Product Owner may decide not to prioritize **anything** the Team's Scrum Master wants or needs.

This problem has been somewhat mitigated in this 2017 Scrum Guide because the Team's Sprint Backlog is required to have (at least) one improvement Story in it (see Annotation 55). This guarantees that at least one Scrum Mastering 'thing' will be done in each Sprint.

Annotation 19: Product Ownership Annotations Summary

We have inserted comments throughout this section, since many of the individual paragraphs are important. Now we'd like to discuss the Product Ownership as a whole...

First, the definition of Team-Product Owner. Using all the 'rewording' that we suggest above, the Scrum Guide defines the Team-Product Owner as:

- The Team member who is accountable for the value of the Development Team's work,

- A Team member who is allowed to do work alongside the rest of the Team, and

- The person who manages the Team-Product Backlog.

Now contrast the Scrum Guide's definition of Team-Product Owner with the following:

- "... report that the Product Owner helps the organization realize value through delivering product solutions that delight customers and users within the constraints of technical feasibility." (from the Scrum Alliance's CSPO LOs, 2017), or

- "The Product Owner is responsible for maximizing return on investment (ROI) by identifying product

> features, translating these into a prioritized list, deciding which should be at the top of the list for the next Sprint, and continually re-prioritizing and refining the list. ... the Product Owner role is similar to the Product Manager or Product Marketing Manager position in many product organizations." (from the Scrum Primer, v2.0, 2012)
>
> It's clear that these two descriptions are about a strategic Product Owner, focused on delivering products to customers and users, while this Scrum Guide (so far, at least) defines a very tactical Team-Product Owner, focused on the value of the Development Team's work (whether it produces Deliverable Results or not).
>
> Even though we haven't seen it yet, these strategic Product Owners also exist in the Scrum Guide, and we'll meet them later.

The Development Team

The Development Team consists of professionals who do the work of delivering a potentially releasable Increment of "Done" product at the end of each Sprint. A "Done" increment is required at the Sprint Review. Only members of the Development Team create the Increment.

> Annotation 20: The Development Team gets work to "Done"
>
> In this paragraph the phrase "potentially useful version of working product" (seen in the previous section) has morphed to become "potentially releasable Increment of 'Done' product". Later on in this Scrum Guide we'll also see the phrase "a 'Done', useable, and potentially releasable

product Increment". So far we don't have the definitions to know what any of these mean, but it seems clear to us that they should mean the same thing. So, here are some definitions from later in this Scrum Guide to help us figure it out:

- "Done" is what it means for work to be complete, and

- The Increment is the accumulated total, across Sprints, of completed, Deliverable, Results.

The expectation is that "Done" is defined well enough so that "Done" work is useful and useable for its intended purpose, and has sufficient quality to be releasable. We also know that it is the Scrum Team that produces the Increment (and the Development Team that builds it), so a potential rewrite of this paragraph is:

> "The Scrum Team consists of professionals who do the work of delivering a "Done" Increment every Sprint, so it can be reviewed. The subset of the Scrum Team that actually creates the Increment (which could include the Product Owner and/or Scrum Master) is called the Development Team."

Development Teams are structured and empowered by the organization to organize and manage their own work. The resulting synergy optimizes the Development Team's overall efficiency and effectiveness.

Annotation 21: Any subset of the Scrum Team must be self-organized

This is basically a restatement that the Scrum Team is self-organized. Since any subset of the (self-organized) Scrum

Team that is working together must, itself, be self-organized. This paragraph also emphasizes that the organization should embrace the Team's self-organization.

Development Teams have the following characteristics:

- They are self-organizing. No one (not even the Scrum Master) tells the Development Team how to turn Product Backlog into Increments of potentially releasable functionality;
- Development Teams are cross-functional, with all the skills as a team necessary to create a product Increment;
- Scrum recognizes no titles for Development Team members, regardless of the work being performed by the person;
- Scrum recognizes no sub-teams in the Development Team, regardless of domains that need to be addressed like testing, architecture, operations, or business analysis; and,
- Individual Development Team members may have specialized skills and areas of focus, but accountability belongs to the Development Team as a whole.

Annotation 22: Scrum Team versus Development Team

This is a nice summary, but the phrase 'Development Team' should probably be replaced by 'Scrum Team'. However, this is a minor quibble, since the Team's Product Owner and Scrum Master might, or might not, be members of the Development Team. There are a few interesting things in here, though:

- Even though the Team's Scrum Master may be part

of the Development Team, they are not a manager, or director of the Development Team.

- Even though the Team-Product Owner and the Team's Scrum Master may act as members of the Development Team, their leadership titles are absent when they are developing – they are simply treated as Team Members as long as they are developing. We like to say that they are not wearing their PO or SM 'hats' when they are on the Development Team.

- Scrum says there are no titles on the Development Team. This does not mean that everybody is treated the same. There may be centers of expertise, there may be mentor/mentee relationships, there may be internal coaching and training – these relationships (and others) are the natural result of the Team's self-organization. The Team's Scrum Master is responsible for facilitating the Scrum Team's self-organization in order to improve the internal workings of the Team.

- Combining this with what was previously defined, the Scrum Guide is saying that the Team-Product Owner is accountable for optimizing the value of the Development Team's work, but the Development Team is accountable for building it.

I'm not sure exactly how this Development Team accountability thing works. We have a few thoughts:

- Our first thought is that there is a mix-up between responsible and accountable, and it should be "responsibility belongs to the Development Team as a whole."

- However, if it means what it says, our second thought is that each member of the Development Team is accountable to the Team-Product Owner (who is not a member of the DevTeam) for getting the work to "Done", and the Team-Product Owner is accountable to people outside the Team (the Business Owner, perhaps) for the value of the work.

- And our third thought is that the Team Product Owner is a member of the DevTeam, and the DevTeam's accountability evidences itself through the Team's Product Owner. That is, the Team's Product Owner represents the accountability of the DevTeam to those outside the Scrum Team that need 'an accounting'.

In any case, we can't see how someone outside the Team can bypass the Team-Product Owner in order to hold the Development Team accountable without upsetting the Team's self-organization...

Development Team Size

Optimal Development Team size is small enough to remain nimble and large enough to complete significant work within a Sprint. Fewer than three Development Team members decrease interaction and results in smaller productivity gains. Smaller Development Teams may encounter skill constraints during the Sprint, causing the Development Team to be unable to deliver a potentially releasable Increment. Having more than nine members requires too much coordination. Large Development Teams generate too much complexity for an empirical process to be useful. The Product Owner and Scrum

Master roles are not included in this count unless they are also executing the work of the Sprint Backlog.

The Scrum Master

The Scrum Master is responsible for promoting and supporting Scrum as defined in the Scrum Guide. Scrum Masters do this by helping everyone understand Scrum theory, practices, rules, and values.

> **Annotation 23: Scrum Masters help interpret and understand the Scrum Guide**
>
> This is an interesting paragraph. Early on we learned that the Scrum Guide is *not* prescriptive, it is guidance that we use as we instantiate Scrum in our Organization. So, this is telling us that the Scrum Master is helping the Organization interpret and understand the Scrum Guide.

The Scrum Master is a servant-leader for the Scrum Team. The Scrum Master helps those outside the Scrum Team understand which of their interactions with the Scrum Team are helpful and which aren't. The Scrum Master helps everyone change these interactions to maximize the value created by the Scrum Team.

> **Annotation 24: Scrum Masters are servant-leaders**
>
> The Scrum Master is a member of the Scrum Team, and this section is written as if there is a single Scrum Team surrounded by Stakeholders. In situations where there are multiple Scrum Teams, or a big Organization with many people surrounding the Scrum Team, your Team's Scrum Master might not be providing all these 'Scrum Master'

> services.
>
> The key thing is that all Scrum Masters are servant-leaders, which means they work to enable and empower people to do their jobs – they work to remove impediments keeping people from being their best.

Scrum Master Service to the Product Owner

The Scrum Master serves the Product Owner in several ways, including:

- Ensuring that goals, scope, and product domain are understood by everyone on the Scrum Team as well as possible;
- Finding techniques for effective Product Backlog management;
- Helping the Scrum Team understand the need for clear and concise Product Backlog items;
- Understanding product planning in an empirical environment;
- Ensuring the Product Owner knows how to arrange the Product Backlog to maximize value;
- Understanding and practicing agility; and,
- Facilitating Scrum events as requested or needed.

Scrum Master Service to the Development Team

The Scrum Master serves the Development Team in several ways, including:

- Coaching the Development Team in self-organization and cross-functionality;
- Helping the Development Team to create high-value products;

- Removing impediments to the Development Team's progress;

Annotation 25: Scrum Masters don't Remove Impediments

Scrum Masters are facilitators, and they facilitate the Team's removal or mitigation of Impediments. It is a common misconception that the Scrum Master is 'on the hook' for removing Impediments, and this lets the Development Team 'off the hook.' We must remember that the complete Scrum Team is self-organized (see Annotation 9), and they are *all* responsible for everything that happens on the Scrum Team.

- Facilitating Scrum events as requested or needed; and,
- Coaching the Development Team in organizational environments in which Scrum is not yet fully adopted and understood.

Annotation 26: The Scrum Master is a Facilitator and Coach

This section is often summarized by saying the Scrum Master 1) Facilitates the Team's self-organization and development, and 2) Coaches the Team in agile practices. We believe the Facilitation part of the job requires the Scrum Master to be with the Team most, if not all, of the time, while the Coaching could be a part-time, as-needed, activity.

(Note: the definition of facilitator used here is the one from Wikipedia: "a person who makes a social process easy or easier." The Scrum Master is not a 'neutral facilitator'; as a Team Member they have a vested interest in the way the Scrum Team works.)

Scrum Master Service to the Organization

The Scrum Master serves the organization in several ways, including:

- Leading and coaching the organization in its Scrum adoption;
- Planning Scrum implementations within the organization;
- Helping employees and stakeholders understand and enact Scrum and empirical product development;
- Causing change that increases the productivity of the Scrum Team; and,
- Working with other Scrum Masters to increase the effectiveness of the application of Scrum in the organization.

Annotation 27: Scrum Masters are Change Agents

This section is often summarized by saying that the Scrum Master is the Organization's Change Agent; coaching the Organization to help it change in order for Scrum to be more successful. In a large Organization, with many Teams (each with its own Scrum Master), it is unlikely that each of them is an Organizational Change Agent. In fact, we believe that the Organization's Change Agent might not on any Scrum Team at all.

If there is a Business Owner setting the Organization's missions, goals, and objectives, the Change Agent kind of Scrum Master is likely working with, and accountable to, the Business Owner to 'improve things'...

Annotation 28: Summary of Scrum Team accountabilities

There is a lot of information in this section about The Scrum Team. Here is a summary of the accountabilities we find in this section. (Remember that we are in the context of a Scrum Team, which consists of a Product Owner, a Scrum Master, and a Development Team.)

The Team-Product Owner:

- Is the Scrum Team Member accountable for maximizing the value of the Development Team's Work;

The Team's Scrum Master:

- Is the Team Member accountable for making sure that Scrum is used correctly, that the Team uses Scrum in a positive way, and that the Team is constantly improving its use of Scrum;
- Facilitates the Team's self-organization and development,
- Coaches the Team in agile practices, and
- Acts as an Organizational Change Agent, as necessary.

The Development Team:

- Consists of the subset of the Scrum Team that actually creates a "Done" Increment every Sprint, which is required in order to be reviewed; and

- Is accountable to for getting the work to "Done," and the Team-Product Owner represents this Accountability outside the Scrum Team.

Scrum Events

Prescribed events are used in Scrum to create regularity and to minimize the need for meetings not defined in Scrum. All events are time-boxed events, such that every event has a maximum duration. Once a Sprint begins, its duration is fixed and cannot be shortened or lengthened. The remaining events may end whenever the purpose of the event is achieved, ensuring an appropriate amount of time is spent without allowing waste in the process.

Other than the Sprint itself, which is a container for all other events, each event in Scrum is a formal opportunity to inspect and adapt something. These events are specifically designed to enable critical transparency and inspection. Failure to include any of these events results in reduced transparency and is a lost opportunity to inspect and adapt.

The Sprint

The heart of Scrum is a Sprint, a time-box of one month or less during which a "Done", useable, and potentially releasable product Increment is created. Sprints have consistent durations throughout a development effort. A new Sprint starts immediately after the conclusion of the previous Sprint.

Sprints contain and consist of the Sprint Planning, Daily Scrums, the development work, the Sprint Review, and the Sprint Retrospective.

During the Sprint:

- No changes are made that would endanger the Sprint Goal;
- Quality goals do not decrease; and,

- Scope may be clarified and re-negotiated between the Product Owner and Development Team as more is learned.

Annotation 29: "Done" and the Sprint Goal are committed to, not the Sprint Backlog

There are two pieces of important information in these three bullets. Since Quality goals are embodied in the definition of "Done" (Annotation 63), the first is that the definition of "Done" won't change during a Sprint. The second is that (even though neither term is defined yet) the Team commits to its Sprint Goal, not its Sprint Backlog. As the first Scrum Guide (2009) said: "The reason for having a Sprint Goal is to give the Team some wiggle room regarding the functionality."

This has two implications: 1) that the Team can be successful without doing all of its Sprint Backlog, and that 2) either the Team-Product Owner or the Development Team is allowed to present new, more important, work to do that will cause a re-plan to occur.

Each Sprint may be considered a project with no more than a one-month horizon. Like projects, Sprints are used to accomplish something. Each Sprint has a goal of what is to be built, a design and flexible plan that will guide building it, the work, and the resultant product increment.

Annotation 30: The Scrum Guide assumes the 'Small Project' strategy

We don't like this paragraph because the strategy of

treating a Sprint as a 'Small Project' is not the only way to do Scrum; we have observed that many Scrum Teams are doing 'Continuous Development'.

When doing Continuous Development, the Backlog represents a Continuous Flow of work for the Team, and the Sprint length is simply the duration until 'inspecting and adapting' the "Done" Results. When doing Continuous Development, the Team relies on Product Ownership to adapt the Backlog (more-or-less continuously) in order to maximize value produced. When the Sprint ends, external Stakeholders review the Sprint's Results in order to help Product Ownership improve how they decide what provides value.

At the beginning of this Scrum Guide, it says that Scrum has been used to "Release products and enhancements, as frequently as many times per day." This is clearly true, as we've all seen it. In many Continuous Development environments, these 'enhancements' are bugs that come flying at the Team in a random, chaotic, fashion, and a typical objective for the Team during a Sprint is something like "fix all the show-stopper bugs that come in and then do whatever other work you have time for." The Team-Product Owner is on the Scrum Team, "Optimizing the value of the work the Development Team performs," and is the one who determines/decides/acknowledges (on the fly) which bugs to fix and whatever other work to do.

Sprints are limited to one calendar month. When a Sprint's horizon is too long the definition of what is being built may change, complexity may rise, and risk may increase. Sprints enable predictability by ensuring inspection and adaptation of progress toward a Sprint Goal at least every calendar month. Sprints also limit risk to one calendar month of cost.

Annotation 31: Sprint Goal Confusion (1)

These previous two paragraphs start a continuing conversation about what the Scrum Guide thinks a Sprint Goal is. There is lots of contradictory and ambiguous information in this Scrum Guide about this topic. These previous two paragraphs both give 'bad advice' about it:

- In the first paragraph, the phrase "Each Sprint has a goal of what is to be built" indicates that the Sprint Goal is a goal about the Results produced during the Sprint – this is not necessarily true, as we'll see later.

- In the second paragraph, the phrase "ensuring inspection and adaptation of progress toward a Sprint Goal at least every calendar month" indicates that the Sprint Goal is something you inspect for across Sprints. This is also not true; the Sprint Goal is something that must be accomplished during the Sprint or the Sprint is considered a 'failed Sprint'.

This second definition is probably a vestige of the days (pre-2011) when the Scrum Guide said there was a Release Goal to move towards across Sprints.

We'll keep going with this discussion about the Sprint Goal as we move along...

Cancelling a Sprint

A Sprint can be cancelled before the Sprint time-box is over. Only the Product Owner has the authority to cancel the Sprint, although he or she may do so under influence from the stakeholders, the Development Team, or the Scrum Master.

A Sprint would be cancelled if the Sprint Goal becomes obsolete. This might occur if the company changes direction or if market or technology conditions change. In general, a Sprint should be cancelled if it no longer makes sense given the circumstances. But, due to the short duration of Sprints, cancellation rarely makes sense.

When a Sprint is cancelled, any completed and "Done" Product Backlog items are reviewed. If part of the work is potentially releasable, the Product Owner typically accepts it. All incomplete Product Backlog Items are re-estimated and put back on the Product Backlog. The work done on them depreciates quickly and must be frequently re-estimated.

Sprint cancellations consume resources, since everyone regroups in another Sprint Planning to start another Sprint. Sprint cancellations are often traumatic to the Scrum Team, and are very uncommon.

Sprint Planning

The work to be performed in the Sprint is planned at the Sprint Planning. This plan is created by the collaborative work of the entire Scrum Team.

Annotation 32: Introduction to Annotations about Planning

The type of planning described in this section is based on the 'Small Project' strategy for a Sprint. In the 'Small Project' strategy there is planning at the beginning of the Sprint to produce a "forecasted Increment" that the Team thinks it can build; and this section describes that kind of planning.

In this section there is lots of confusion of what a Sprint Goal is. As we'll see eventually, the Sprint Goal is something that the Scrum Team derives and commits to, defines success for the Sprint, and could be unconnected to the Results produced. However, there are many places in the Scrum Guide that (incorrectly) imply that the Sprint Goal is the based on the "forecasted Increment" – and we will point them out.

Sprint Planning is time-boxed to a maximum of eight hours for a one-month Sprint. For shorter Sprints, the event is usually shorter. The Scrum Master ensures that the event takes place and that attendants understand its purpose. The Scrum Master teaches the Scrum Team to keep it within the time-box.

Sprint Planning answers the following:

- What can be delivered in the Increment resulting from the upcoming Sprint?
- How will the work needed to deliver the Increment be achieved?

Topic One: What can be done this Sprint?

The Development Team works to forecast the functionality that will be developed during the Sprint. The Product Owner discusses the objective that the Sprint should achieve and the Product Backlog items that, if completed in the Sprint, would achieve the Sprint Goal. The entire Scrum Team collaborates on understanding the work of the Sprint.

Annotation 33: Sprint Goal Confusion (2)

The most important thing in this paragraph is that the Team *forecasts* what will be developed, it does not *commit* to what will be developed. The idea of forecasting versus committing is one of the big ideas in the first Scrum Guide, in 2009.

In fact, the Sprint Goal was introduced in 2009 in order to have something the Team could commit to besides the functionality that would (or could) be developed during the Sprint. The first Scrum Guide said: "The reason for having a Sprint Goal is to give the Team some wiggle room regarding the functionality." The idea was that committing to *complete* all the work may cause the Team to rush to complete it, making Quality the variable – and it shouldn't be. By having a Sprint Goal to commit to, the Team can find a way to successfully accomplish its Sprint without compromising the Quality of the completed Backlog Items.

We see the writers of the Scrum Guide struggling with the concept of a Sprint Goal throughout this 2017 Scrum Guide. In this first paragraph, for example, the Team-Product Owner 'brings in' "an objective that the Sprint should achieve" and seems to confuse this with the Sprint Goal the Team should commit to. This seems to violate that whole "wiggle room" thing the Sprint Goal is for…

It's certainly ok for the Team-Product Owner to bring in objectives they want met in the Sprint. However, the Team must be value-driven and realize that these objectives are merely inputs to Sprint Planning, not things to commit to.

The input to this meeting is the Product Backlog, the latest product Increment, projected capacity of the Development Team during the Sprint, and past performance of the Development Team. The number of items selected from the Product Backlog for the Sprint is solely up to the Development Team. Only the Development Team can assess what it can accomplish over the upcoming Sprint.

> ### Annotation 34: Expect the unexpected
>
> Actually, given that there are likely to be unforeseen impediments that appear in the Sprint, not even the "Development Team can assess what it can accomplish over the upcoming Sprint." There is often a significant amount of discovery during a Sprint. Be prepared to "inspect and adapt" early and often – at every level of work detail.

During Sprint Planning the Scrum Team also crafts a Sprint Goal. The Sprint Goal is an objective that will be met within the Sprint through the implementation of the Product Backlog, and it provides guidance to the Development Team on why it is building the Increment.

> ### Annotation 35: Sprint Goal Confusion (3)
>
> Here we see another attempt at providing a definition of the Sprint Goal; it is something that "provides guidance to the Development Team on why it is building the Increment." Now, the default Sprint Goal: "We will have something to Review this Sprint," fits this definition, but in general, this isn't correct – as we'll see later.

Topic Two: How will the chosen work get done?

Having set the Sprint Goal and selected the Product Backlog items for the Sprint, the Development Team decides how it will build this functionality into a "Done" product Increment during the Sprint. The Product Backlog items selected for this Sprint plus the plan for delivering them is called the Sprint Backlog.

Annotation 36: The 'Small Project' strategy requires a forecast

Note that this paragraph really gives the 'we know what we're delivering and how we're doing it' vibe, doesn't it? It seems like the Scrum Guide, in spite of itself, is requiring a commitment to the forecast the Team comes up with. It goes along with the statement "Only the Development Team can assess what it can accomplish over the upcoming Sprint," that we see above.

But, we know that it's not the Team's job to know how much it will deliver, right? The Team's job is to assure that any work they complete is actually "Done," and the Sprint Goal gives them the "wiggle room" they need to enable them to focus on doing that.

The Development Team usually starts by designing the system and the work needed to convert the Product Backlog into a working product Increment. Work may be of varying size, or estimated effort. However, enough work is planned during Sprint Planning for the Development Team to forecast what it believes it can do in the upcoming Sprint. Work planned for the first days of the Sprint by the Development Team is decomposed by the end of this meeting, often to units of one day or less. The Development Team self-organizes to undertake the work in the Sprint Backlog, both during Sprint Planning and as needed throughout the Sprint.

The Product Owner can help to clarify the selected Product Backlog items and make trade-offs. If the Development Team determines it has too much or too little work, it may renegotiate the selected Product Backlog items with the Product Owner. The Development Team may also invite other people to attend to provide technical or domain advice.

By the end of the Sprint Planning, the Development Team should be able to explain to the Product Owner and Scrum Master how it intends to work as a self-organizing team to accomplish the Sprint Goal and create the anticipated Increment.

Annotation 37: The 'Small Project' strategy anticipates what it will produce

In this, the second part of project-style planning, the Team (including the Team-Product Owner) collaborates to come up with a plan for creating an Increment. They analyze, estimate, collaborate, and so on, until they feel confident enough to forecast what Increment it believes it can do in the upcoming Sprint. At the end of Sprint Planning, there will be a Sprint Backlog outlining how the Team intends to deliver the "anticipated Increment" and achieve the Sprint Goal.

The notion of a "forecasted/anticipated Increment" really points out that this is all about the 'small project' strategy of agile development. In this strategy, there are two parts of the Sprint Backlog:

1. There is a plan for achieving the "forecasted/ anticipated Increment", and

2. There is a Sprint Goal to 'fall back on' if the "forecasted/anticipated Increment" is not achieved.

Because the purpose of the Sprint Goal is "to give the Team some 'wiggle room' regarding the functionality," the Sprint Goal may not be to 'achieve the forecasted/anticipated Increment.' It must be something the Team feels confident it can achieve, and achieving the Sprint Goal is

---

what defines success for the Sprint – not building the "forecasted/anticipated Increment." The Sprint Goal is what enables agility and keeps the Sprint from becoming a march to achieve the "forecasted/anticipated Increment."

As we'll see later in this Scrum Guide (see Annotation 55), the Sprint Backlog is also required to contain "at least one high priority process improvement identified in the previous Retrospective meeting." These 'improvement' work items are typically called Kaizens, from the Japanese word for continuous improvement (or good change).

The requirement for a Kaizen was added in this 2017 Scrum Guide, and the fact that it is not mentioned in the Sprint Planning portion of the Guide is clearly a bug that needs to be fixed – but it's no big deal.

Sprint Goal

The Sprint Goal is an objective set for the Sprint that can be met through the implementation of Product Backlog. It provides guidance to the Development Team on why it is building the Increment. It is created during the Sprint Planning meeting. The Sprint Goal gives the Development Team some flexibility regarding the functionality implemented within the Sprint. The selected Product Backlog items deliver one coherent function, which can be the Sprint Goal. The Sprint Goal can be any other coherence that causes the Development Team to work together rather than on separate initiatives.

Annotation 38: Sprint Goal Confusion ended

There are two sentences in this paragraph that finally tell us what the Sprint Goal is all about. First, there is a version of the "wiggle room" statement we mentioned before: "The Sprint Goal gives the Development Team some flexibility regarding the functionality implemented within the Sprint." And, second, we have a description of what the Sprint Goal is: "The Sprint Goal can be any ... coherence that causes the Development Team to work together rather than on separate initiatives." This finally gives us what we need, and here is our final description of the Sprint Goal:

> "The Sprint Goal is something the Scrum Team members agree to accomplish *together* within the Sprint. The Sprint Goal defines success for the Sprint, and committing to the Sprint Goal, rather than the Sprint Backlog, allows the Team the 'wiggle room' needed to avoid compromising Quality while it works on the Sprint Backlog."

As the Development Team works, it keeps the Sprint Goal in mind. In order to satisfy the Sprint Goal, it implements functionality and technology. If the work turns out to be different than the Development Team expected, they collaborate with the Product Owner to negotiate the scope of Sprint Backlog within the Sprint.

Annotation 39: Working towards the Sprint Goal

With this new understanding of the Sprint Goal, I would rewrite this paragraph as:

> "As the Development Team works, it does whatever it needs to do in order to satisfy the Sprint Goal. If the scope of the Sprint Backlog needs to change, the Development Team collaborates with the Team-Product Owner to re-negotiate the scope of the Sprint Backlog within the Sprint, as long as it does not force

> the Sprint Goal to change."

Note: If re-negotiating the Scope of the Sprint Backlog *will* cause the Sprint Goal to change, it might be a good reason for the Team-Product Owner to **Cancel the Sprint** and re-plan.

Annotation 40: Sprint Planning using the 'Continuous Development' strategy

The previous few pages described a form of Sprint Planning to be used when treating the Sprint as a 'Small Project'. This is probably a good thing to do when using that development strategy. However, we often see the 'Continuous Development' strategy used, which changes how we do planning. In a nutshell, here what Sprint Planning looks like while using the 'continuous development' strategy:

> Sprint Planning is a collaborative effort of the entire Scrum Team, and should take no more than 1-2 hours. The Inputs to Sprint Planning are 1) the Team-Product Backlog, 2) any objectives the Team-Product Owner has, and 3) the Team's past performance. The Outputs from Sprint Planning are: 1) Sprint End (the date/time for the Sprint Review), 2) the Sprint Goal, 3) the Sprint's Kaizen (as part of the Sprint Backlog), and 4) an appropriate amount of Sprint Backlog, as defined by the Team.

When using this sort of Sprint Planning, the Sprint Backlog is not committed to, and there is no forecast. The Team knows that it doesn't know what (or how much) work it will complete; it is relying on the Team-Product Owner, not the

Sprint Backlog, to drive development during the Sprint. In many cases the Sprint Backlog has just enough Items to get the Team moving, and additional planning is essentially continuous throughout the Sprint (in this case the development is very lean, mimicking continuous flow).

Daily Scrum

The Daily Scrum is a 15-minute time-boxed event for the Development Team. The Daily Scrum is held every day of the Sprint. At it, the Development Team plans work for the next 24 hours. This optimizes team collaboration and performance by inspecting the work since the last Daily Scrum and forecasting upcoming Sprint work. The Daily Scrum is held at the same time and place each day to reduce complexity.

The Development Team uses the Daily Scrum to inspect progress toward the Sprint Goal and to inspect how progress is trending toward completing the work in the Sprint Backlog. The Daily Scrum optimizes the probability that the Development Team will meet the Sprint Goal. Every day, the Development Team should understand how it intends to work together as a self-organizing team to accomplish the Sprint Goal and create the anticipated Increment by the end of the Sprint.

Annotation 41: Separation of Sprint Goal and Sprint Backlog in Daily Scrum

The Daily Scrum is a daily 'inspect and adapt' conversation to re-plan the work that going on in two areas: 1) how are we doing on the Sprint Goal? and 2) how are we doing on the Sprint Backlog? This separation of the two topics shows that our interpretation of what the Sprint Goal is was correct; the Sprint Goal need not be linked to either the Sprint

Backlog or the Increment being produced.

The structure of the meeting is set by the Development Team and can be conducted in different ways if it focuses on progress toward the Sprint Goal. Some Development Teams will use questions, some will be more discussion based. Here is an example of what might be used:

- What did I do yesterday that helped the Development Team meet the Sprint Goal?
- What will I do today to help the Development Team meet the Sprint Goal?
- Do I see any impediment that prevents me or the Development Team from meeting the Sprint Goal?

The Development Team or team members often meet immediately after the Daily Scrum for detailed discussions, or to adapt, or replan, the rest of the Sprint's work.

The Scrum Master ensures that the Development Team has the meeting, but the Development Team is responsible for conducting the Daily Scrum. The Scrum Master teaches the Development Team to keep the Daily Scrum within the 15-minute time-box.

The Daily Scrum is an internal meeting for the Development Team. If others are present, the Scrum Master ensures that they do not disrupt the meeting.

Daily Scrums improve communications, eliminate other meetings, identify impediments to development for removal, highlight and promote quick decision-making, and improve the Development Team's level of knowledge. This is a key inspect and adapt meeting.

62

> **Annotation 42: The three questions are no longer dogma**
>
> The most important thing in this section is a change that was made in this 2017 Scrum Guide; the questions are no longer dogma. The addition of the phrase: "The structure of the meeting is set by the Development Team and can be conducted in different ways" clarifies what many have believed for years – that the format of the Daily Scrum is up the Team as a self-organization issue. The important thing is that the Team meets daily to determine what it hopes to do today in order to: 1) meet the Sprint Goal, and 2) accomplish the work in the Sprint Backlog – it is a very tactical (not strategic) meeting.

Sprint Review

A Sprint Review is held at the end of the Sprint to inspect the Increment and adapt the Product Backlog if needed. During the Sprint Review, the Scrum Team and stakeholders collaborate about what was done in the Sprint. Based on that and any changes to the Product Backlog during the Sprint, attendees collaborate on the next things that could be done to optimize value. This is an informal meeting, not a status meeting, and the presentation of the Increment is intended to elicit feedback and foster collaboration.

This is at most a four-hour meeting for one-month Sprints. For shorter Sprints, the event is usually shorter. The Scrum Master ensures that the event takes place and that attendees understand its purpose. The Scrum Master teaches everyone involved to keep it within the time-box.

> **Annotation 43: The Sprint Review may not be the only feedback**
>
> Feedback is the lifeblood of agility, and Scrum has a formal Review meeting to help supply this feedback. This meeting may not be enough; it is just the *formal* meeting that *must* take place. Sometimes it takes more than just a few hours to get all the feedback you need. Therefore, be prepared to have Backlog Items in the next Sprint whose goal is to gather additional feedback on specific items. These Backlog Items are usually time-boxed and focused on specific issues or features that need further review and feedback from Stakeholders and Subject Matter Experts. These Backlog Items are one kind of non-developmental work we find in a Team-Product Backlog (Team Work Backlog), as we discussed in the "The Product Owner" section.
>
> **Note**: We have rearranged the following list to make it plain that there are two sublists with different foci.

The Sprint Review includes the following elements:

- Attendees include the Scrum Team and key stakeholders invited by the Product Owner;
- The Product Owner explains what Product Backlog items have been "Done" and what has not been "Done";
- The Development Team discusses what went well during the Sprint, what problems it ran into, and how those problems were solved;
- The Development Team demonstrates the work that it has "Done" and answers questions about the Increment;

- The entire group collaborates on what to do next, so that the Sprint Review provides valuable input to subsequent Sprint Planning;

Annotation 44: The Sprint Review has a tactical part

This first part of the list is about Reviewing the work that was "Done" within the Sprint. The object is to have a collaborative discussion between Development Team Members who built the Product, and Stakeholders who care about the features and capabilities of the Product. This discussion is about what is "Done" so far (with specific focus on what was "Done" in *this* Sprint), and what should be worked on next. The discussion focuses on the questions: "What do you like?" "What don't you like?" "What should we do next?" and the like. This part of the Review is fairly tactical and focused on development of the Product.

- The Product Owner discusses the Product Backlog as it stands. He or she projects likely target and delivery dates based on progress to date (if needed);
- Review of how the marketplace or potential use of the product might have changed what is the most valuable thing to do next; and
- Review of the timeline, budget, potential capabilities, and marketplace for the next anticipated releases of functionality or capability of the product.

Annotation 45: The Sprint Review has a strategic part

The second part of the list is a 'higher-level', more strategic, discussion between Product Ownership and Stakeholders who care about Dates, Dollars, and the overall direction of

---

the effort. The purpose of this part of the Review is to modify Release Goals, update Release Plans, change projected delivery dates, and so on.

Most, if not all, Development Team members are not necessary for this discussion, and (in my opinion) it is often harmful if they are there. In my experience, this part of the Review often includes a discussion about the Team's capabilities (too slow, too inefficient, etc.) and this discussion could be very harmful to the Team. For example, if Team Members feel that they are too slow they may try to speed up by cutting corners, and not getting their work all the way to "Done" – and this can be disastrous for the Product itself.

This part of the Review is strategic, and focused on future planning and direction. Because of this, we believe that it is more for the Product-Product Owner than the Scrum Team (see Annotation 49 for discussion of the Product-Product Owner).

The result of the Sprint Review is a revised Product Backlog that defines the probable Product Backlog items for the next Sprint. The Product Backlog may also be adjusted overall to meet new opportunities.

Sprint Retrospective

The Sprint Retrospective is an opportunity for the Scrum Team to inspect itself and create a plan for improvements to be enacted during the next Sprint.

The Sprint Retrospective occurs after the Sprint Review and prior to the next Sprint Planning. This is at most a three-hour meeting for one-month Sprints. For shorter Sprints, the event is usually shorter. The Scrum Master ensures that the event takes place and that attendants understand its purpose.

The Scrum Master ensures that the meeting is positive and productive. The Scrum Master teaches all to keep it within the time-box. The Scrum Master participates as a peer team member in the meeting from the accountability over the Scrum process.

Annotation 46: Team's Scrum Master accountable for the Team's Scrum Mastering

Earlier in the annotations (see Annotation 16), I indicated that the Team's Scrum Master is accountable for the Team's Scrum Mastering. Right here, in the previous paragraph, where it says: "The Scrum Master participates as a peer team member in the meeting from the accountability over the Scrum process." is where the Scrum Guide indicates that is true.

The purpose of the Sprint Retrospective is to:

- Inspect how the last Sprint went with regards to people, relationships, process, and tools;
- Identify and order the major items that went well and potential improvements; and,
- Create a plan for implementing improvements to the way the Scrum Team does its work.

Annotation 47: The Retrospective is for the Scrum Team to improve itself

The Retrospective is about improving the way the Scrum Team works, which includes improvements in Development, Scrum Mastering, and Product Ownership.

The Team-Product Owner participates as a peer team member for three reasons: 1) as the primary participant in Product Ownership, 2) based on his/her accountability for optimizing the value of the Development Team's work, and 3) as a potential member of the Development Team.

The Scrum Master participates as a peer team member for three reasons: 1) as the primary participant in Scrum Mastering, 2) because of his/her accountability to help the Team/Organization interpret and understand the Scrum Process, and 3) as a potential member of the Development Team.

The Scrum Master encourages the Scrum Team to improve, within the Scrum process framework, its development process and practices to make it more effective and enjoyable for the next Sprint. During each Sprint Retrospective, the Scrum Team plans ways to increase product quality by improving work processes or adapting the definition of "Done", if appropriate and not in conflict with product or organizational standards.

Annotation 48: Confusion between Scrum Team and Development Team

In this paragraph either: 1) the term "Scrum Team" should be replaced by "Development Team", or 2) the words "development process and practices to make it more..." should be replaced with "processes and practices to make them more..."

We must remember that the Team-Product Owner is accountable for optimizing the value of the Development Team's work, and this fact can lead to some contention in this part of the Retrospective. It is not unusual for the

Team-Product Owner and the rest of the Team to have different ideas of 'how good is good enough' when it comes to product quality – and we've seen it go both ways.

It is up to the Scrum Master to 'referee' these discussions and make sure any resulting modifications to the definition of "Done" are visible to appropriate Stakeholders.

By the end of the Sprint Retrospective, the Scrum Team should have identified improvements that it will implement in the next Sprint. Implementing these improvements in the next Sprint is the adaptation to the inspection of the Scrum Team itself. Although improvements may be implemented at any time, the Sprint Retrospective provides a formal opportunity to focus on inspection and adaptation.

Scrum Artifacts

Scrum's artifacts represent work or value to provide transparency and opportunities for inspection and adaptation. Artifacts defined by Scrum are specifically designed to maximize transparency of key information so that everybody has the same understanding of the artifact.

Product Backlog

The Product Backlog is an ordered list of everything that is known to be needed in the product. It is the single source of requirements for any changes to be made to the product. The Product Owner is responsible for the Product Backlog, including its content, availability, and ordering.

A Product Backlog is never complete. The earliest development of it lays out the initially known and best-understood requirements. The Product Backlog evolves as the product and the environment in which it will be used evolves. The Product Backlog is dynamic; it constantly changes to identify what the product needs to be appropriate, competitive, and useful. If a product exists, its Product Backlog also exists.

> **Annotation 49: Every Product has a Product Backlog and a Product Owner**
>
> Note the sentence: "If a product exists, its Product Backlog also exists," as it's important. It should be clear that a Team-Product (the totality of the Deliverable Results of a single Scrum Team's Development Team) is not the only kind of product that there is – any product that is worked on by more than one Team is not a Team-Product, and any product that is not the only thing a Team works on is not a Team-Product. Therefore, there are Product Backlogs that are not Team-Product Backlogs, and they are associated with products other than Team-Products. Each of these Product Backlogs is "an ordered list of everything that is known to be needed in the product."
>
> We should think of such a Product (one that is not necessarily a Team-Product) as a Deliverable the Organization is providing to Stakeholders, and its Product Backlog as a list of reviewable pieces of those deliverables. Some Products are worked on by many Scrum Teams, and some Scrum Teams work on multiple Products.
>
> If the Product *is* the totality of a single Scrum Team's deliverables, then the Product may also be a Team-Product, and the Product Backlog consists of the portion of the Team-Product Backlog that consists of the Development Team's Deliverable Results (see Annotation 11).
>
> And, in the first paragraph of this section we see the

sentence: "The Product Owner is responsible for the Product Backlog, including its content, availability, and ordering." In other words, each of these non-Team-Products also has its own Product Owner. I think it is safe to infer that this type of Product Owner is also accountable for maximizing the value of the associated Product, even though it's not explicitly stated anywhere (that I can find) within this Scrum Guide.

We will use the terms 'Product-Product", "Product-Product Backlog", and Product-Product Owner for the non-Team ones, because we need to keep them separate somehow.

Annotation 50: There are two types of Products in the 2017 Scrum Guide

So, there are two kinds of Products, Product Backlogs, and Product Owners implicit in this Scrum Guide. Let me list what we know so far:

- There are Team-Products, each of which is the totality of a single Scrum Team's Deliverables Results that are produced by the Development Team's work (Annotation 11);

- Each Scrum Team has a Team-Product Backlog that includes all the work the Scrum Team will work on next, not just the Deliverable-producing work, and the Team-Product Backlog should (more correctly) be called the Team Work Backlog (Annotation 15).

- Each Scrum Team has a Team-Product Owner, who is the Scrum Team Member who is accountable for making sure the work gets to "Done" (including

Quality), maximizing the value of the Development Team's Work, whether the work produces Deliverable Results or not (Annotation 14), and who manages the Team-Product Backlog (Team Work Backlog) (Annotation 13).

- There are Product-Products, which are anything the Organization considers to be a Product that will be delivered to Stakeholders. It is possible that a Product-Product is also a Team-Product, if it consists of the totality of a single Scrum Team's Deliverable Results that are produced by the Development Team's work (Annotation 49);

- Each Product-Product has a Product-Product Backlog, which is an ordered list of everything that is known to be needed in the Product-Product; if the Product-Product is also a Team-Product, the Product-Product Backlog could be imbedded within the Team-Product Backlog, (the Team Work Backlog) (Annotation 49);

- Each Product-Product has a Product-Product Owner, who is accountable for maximizing the value of the Product-Product, and is responsible for the associated Product-Product Backlog, including its content, availability, and ordering (Annotation 49).

The next few paragraphs are clearly talking about Product-Product Backlogs, not Team-Product Backlogs.

The Product Backlog lists all features, functions, requirements, enhancements, and fixes that constitute the changes to be made to the product in future releases. Product Backlog items have the attributes of a description, order, estimate, and value.

Product Backlog items often include test descriptions that will prove its completeness when "Done."

As a product is used and gains value, and the marketplace provides feedback, the Product Backlog becomes a larger and more exhaustive list. Requirements never stop changing, so a Product Backlog is a living artifact. Changes in business requirements, market conditions, or technology may cause changes in the Product Backlog.

Multiple Scrum Teams often work together on the same product. One Product Backlog is used to describe the upcoming work on the product. A Product Backlog attribute that groups items may then be employed.

Annotation 51: A simple scaling problem

In this previous paragraph we see the Scrum Guide expose a scaling problem without providing a solution. However, we already have enough information to know what this paragraph means:

1. It is clear that it is saying that multiple Scrum Teams can work on the same Product-Product, because it's not a "Product resulting from work of [a single Scrum Team's] Development Team."

2. The Product-Product has its own Product-Product Backlog (consisting of deliverable Backlog items), and its own Product-Product Owner.

3. Each of the Teams has its own Team-Product, its own Team-Product Backlog, and its own Team-Product Owner.

So, if there are two Scrum Teams working on the same Product-Product, there is a flow of work with items flowing

---

from the one Product-Product Backlog to the two Team-Product Backlogs, and three Product Owners managing this flow. As we've seen before, this SG insists that these POs are actually people, so there could be 1-3 people involved, divvying up the Product Ownership in some way.

But there is a significant philosophical issue: "How many Teams can a single person be the TPO for?" which leads to some serious discussions about what a Team's self-organization actually means. Clearly, if one of my Team's people is also on another team, this puts a constraint on what my team can do in terms of its self-organization. How big can this constraint be before my team can no longer be said to be self-organized? In the text prior to Annotation 9, we see the definition that self-organized teams "choose how best to accomplish their work, rather than being directed by others outside the team." When does an external constraint become so serious that it can be construed as "direction"? I think that these questions are unanswerable, but most people agree that being a TPO for more than 'a few' Teams is impossible, where 'a few' is between 2 and 8, depending on who you are talking to.

Anyway...

By reading some of Ken Schwaber's previous books ("*Agile Project Management with Scrum*" and "*The Enterprise and Scrum*"), it is clear where this SG paragraph comes from. In these books we see a single Product-Product Backlog that represents *all* the work for a Product-Product (not just the deliverable work), and a grouping mechanism that allows each Scrum Team to 'view' its part of the overall Backlog. In other words, each Team-Product Backlog is a subset of (or imbedded in) the overall Product-Product Backlog.

Each of these imbedded Team-Product Backlogs is managed by the appropriate Team-Product Owner and refined by his/her Team in order to make its items "Ready" for development. This process of Refinement is described and defined in the following paragraphs, which transition back to talking about a single Development Team with its associated Team-Product Owner and Team-Product Backlog (Team Work Backlog).

Product Backlog refinement is the act of adding detail, estimates, and order to items in the Product Backlog. This is an ongoing process in which the Product Owner and the Development Team collaborate on the details of Product Backlog items. During Product Backlog refinement, items are reviewed and revised. The Scrum Team decides how and when refinement is done. Refinement usually consumes no more than 10% of the capacity of the Development Team. However, Product Backlog items can be updated at any time by the Product Owner or at the Product Owner's discretion.

Higher ordered Product Backlog items are usually clearer and more detailed than lower ordered ones. More precise estimates are made based on the greater clarity and increased detail; the lower the order, the less detail. Product Backlog items that will occupy the Development Team for the upcoming Sprint are refined so that any one item can reasonably be "Done" within the Sprint time-box. Product Backlog items that can be "Done" by the Development Team within one Sprint are deemed "Ready" for selection in a Sprint Planning. Product Backlog items usually acquire this degree of transparency through the above described refining activities.

Annotation 52: A Scrum Team Refines its Team Work Backlog

This discussion of Refinement is about a single Team refining its Team-Product Backlog (Team Work Backlog). Clearly, might need to be some 'higher' level of Refinement that takes the items in an higher-level Product-Product Backlog and refines them until they are appropriate to 'hand off' to an individual Scrum Team. Once the Scrum Team gets the items, they further refine them until they are "Ready" to work on. This is clearly a scaling issue, but so is this whole issue of Product-Product Backlogs versus Team-Product Backlogs.

The Development Team is responsible for all estimates. The Product Owner may influence the Development Team by helping it understand and select trade-offs, but the people who will perform the work make the final estimate.

Monitoring Progress Toward Goals

At any point in time, the total work remaining to reach a goal can be summed. The Product Owner tracks this total work remaining at least every Sprint Review. The Product Owner compares this amount with work remaining at previous Sprint Reviews to assess progress toward completing projected work by the desired time for the goal. This information is made transparent to all stakeholders.

Various projective practices upon trending have been used to forecast progress, like burn-downs, burn-ups, or cumulative flows. These have proven useful. However, these do not replace the importance of empiricism. In complex environments, what will happen is unknown. Only what has already happened may be used for forward-looking decision-making.

Annotation 53: Product-Product Owners make projections

It's important to be able to guesstimate when a Team will reach an objective, but it's clearly *more* important to be able to predict when a Product-Product can be delivered to its users. This would imply that these projections are done more by Product-Product Owners than Team-Product Owners. This is a hard problem, and this discussion only scratches the surface...

As part of this scratching, we can see that the second sub-list of things that happen in a Sprint Review is also something a Product-Product Owner might do, rather than a Team-Product Owner. Go back and take a look at the sub-list above Annotation 45...

Sprint Backlog

The Sprint Backlog is the set of Product Backlog items selected for the Sprint, plus a plan for delivering the product Increment and realizing the Sprint Goal. The Sprint Backlog is a forecast by the Development Team about what functionality will be in the next Increment and the work needed to deliver that functionality into a "Done" Increment.

Annotation 54: Comments on the Sprint backlog...

Now, this is really nice for a couple of reasons:

- It has cleanly separated the product Increment from the Sprint Goal, and

---

- It clearly states that the Sprint Backlog is a forecast, not a commitment.

And it's not so good for a couple of others:

- It is locked into the 'Small Project' strategy, talking about "what functionality will be in the next Increment", and

- As we'll see in the next paragraph, it's not just about the Increment and the Sprint Goal; it's also about the Kaizen (process improvement work item).

The Sprint Backlog makes visible all the work that the Development Team identifies as necessary to meet the Sprint Goal. To ensure continuous improvement, it includes at least one high priority process improvement identified in the previous Retrospective meeting.

Annotation 55: There is at least one Kaizen in each Sprint.

We refer to this "high priority process improvement" item as a Kaizen, which is a Japanese word that means 'continuous improvement'. Note that the Kaizen originates in the previous Retrospective meeting, which means that the Scrum Master and the Scrum Team (including the Team-Product Owner) agreed should it be done.

There are two things of interest here:

1. It is new in this Scrum Guide that every Sprint must have a Kaizen, and this is a very good thing.

2. The Sprint is not just about the Sprint Goal; it's also about the Increment and the Kaizen; but the Sprint Goal is what defines success for the Sprint (note

> that achieving the Kaizen could be the Sprint Goal).

The Sprint Backlog is a plan with enough detail that changes in progress can be understood in the Daily Scrum. The Development Team modifies the Sprint Backlog throughout the Sprint, and the Sprint Backlog emerges during the Sprint. This emergence occurs as the Development Team works through the plan and learns more about the work needed to achieve the Sprint Goal.

As new work is required, the Development Team adds it to the Sprint Backlog. As work is performed or completed, the estimated remaining work is updated. When elements of the plan are deemed unnecessary, they are removed. Only the Development Team can change its Sprint Backlog during a Sprint. The Sprint Backlog is a highly visible, real-time picture of the work that the Development Team plans to accomplish during the Sprint, and it belongs solely to the Development Team.

> **Annotation 56: The Sprint Backlog is a 'living document'**
>
> This is a wonderful paragraph, except for the second sentence, which is confusing until you remember that the plan being discussed is "for delivering the product Increment and realizing the Sprint Goal [and the Kaizen]." This whole paragraph is simply trying to say that the Sprint Backlog is a 'living document' and the Development Team changes it as necessary.

Monitoring Sprint Progress

At any point in time in a Sprint, the total work remaining in the Sprint Backlog can be summed. The Development Team tracks this total work remaining at least for every Daily Scrum to project the likelihood of achieving the Sprint Goal. By tracking the remaining work throughout the Sprint, the Development Team can manage its progress.

Annotation 57: A terrible description of measuring progress

In my opinion, this paragraph is terrible, for lots of reasons:

- It assumes that the Sprint Goal means 'achieve all the work we planned',

- It assumes that the Sprint is completely planned out, so there is the notion of 'total work remaining', even though we just said that the Sprint Backlog is emergent,

- It puts the focus on total work remaining instead of getting current work to "Done",

- It assumes that we measure progress as 'how close to our objective are we' rather than 'how much work have we got done', and finally,

- We are back to the notion that the Sprint is a time-boxed container and all the work in the container must be finished, thus encouraging Quality to become the variable... bad idea.

Increment

The Increment is the sum of all the Product Backlog items completed during a Sprint and the value of the increments of all previous Sprints. At the end of a Sprint, the new Increment must be "Done," which means it must be in useable condition and meet the Scrum Team's definition of "Done." An increment is a body of inspectable, done work that supports empiricism at the end of the Sprint. The increment is a step toward a vision or goal. The increment must be in useable condition regardless of whether the Product Owner decides to release it.

Annotation 58: Analysis of the definition of "Increment"

The word "Increment" is short for "Product Increment", and this is only about deliverable Backlog Items. The non-deliverable ones don't need to be reviewed by external Stakeholders...

Since "Done" is what it means for work to be completed, a lot of this paragraph simply collapses to "The Increment is the sum, across Sprints, of "Done," deliverable, Backlog Items." As we've said before, the expectation is that "Done" is defined well enough so that "Done" work is useful and useable for its intended purpose, and has sufficient quality to be releasable.

So, this paragraph is saying that an Increment is useful if it:

- Is inspectable, supporting empiricism at the end of the Sprint, and

- Is a step towards a vision or goal.

This seems reasonable to us... as long as we realize that the vision or goal could be very amorphous, like "make progress" or "move forward," and is not necessarily the same as the Sprint Goal. After all, we need to be able to gather meaningful feedback, and we should be going somewhere...

Artifact Transparency

Scrum relies on transparency. Decisions to optimize value and control risk are made based on the perceived state of the artifacts. To the extent that transparency is complete, these decisions have a sound basis. To the extent that the artifacts are incompletely transparent, these decisions can be flawed, value may diminish and risk may increase.

The Scrum Master must work with the Product Owner, Development Team, and other involved parties to understand if the artifacts are completely transparent. There are practices for coping with incomplete transparency; the Scrum Master must help everyone apply the most appropriate practices in the absence of complete transparency. A Scrum Master can detect incomplete transparency by inspecting the artifacts, sensing patterns, listening closely to what is being said, and detecting differences between expected and real results.

The Scrum Master's job is to work with the Scrum Team and the organization to increase the transparency of the artifacts. This work usually involves learning, convincing, and change. Transparency doesn't occur overnight, but is a path.

Annotation 59: Analysis of Comments on Transparency

What these three paragraphs are trying to say is pretty simple:

1. To the extent that an artifact isn't actually what you think it is, any adaptations you make based on inspecting the artifact are flawed, and

2. It is the Scrum Master's job to do whatever is necessary to insure that people inspecting artifacts

82

> see them as they really are.
>
> This section is simply a lead-in to the following discussion of the definition of "Done", as one of the primary questions when reviewing the Increment is: 'Ok, so this thing is "Done"… what does that actually mean?'

Definition of "Done"

When a Product Backlog item or an Increment is described as "Done", everyone must understand what "Done" means. Although this may vary significantly per Scrum Team, members must have a shared understanding of what it means for work to be complete, to ensure transparency. This is the definition of "Done" for the Scrum Team and is used to assess when work is complete on the product Increment.

> **Annotation 60: Definition of "Done"**
>
> This paragraph states that "everyone must understand what "Done" means." Who is this everyone? From a simple reading of this paragraph you might think that "everyone" means everyone on the Scrum Team, but you'd be wrong. Way back in the beginning of this Scrum Guide it says: "Those performing the work and those inspecting the resulting increment must share a common definition of 'Done'", so we know that "everyone" actually means everyone building or reviewing the Increment (Annotation 4). Therefore, we can define "Done" by:
>
>> "The common understanding between the Team and Stakeholders, of what it means for a Product Backlog Item or Increment to be complete."
>
> Also, since the Increment "is the sum of all deliverable

Product Backlog items completed during a Sprint and the value of the increments of all previous Sprints," it should be clear that "Done" for an Increment must mean that every Backlog Item included in that Increment must be "Done" as well. This leads to the conclusion that once a "not Done" Item is included in an Increment, the Increment can never be "Done" until that Item is cleaned up. It's an instance of the aphorism "one bad apple spoils the barrel," I think...

The same definition guides the Development Team in knowing how many Product Backlog items it can select during a Sprint Planning. The purpose of each Sprint is to deliver Increments of potentially releasable functionality that adhere to the Scrum Team's current definition of "Done."

Annotation 61: Effort is based on how hard it is to get to "Done"

The Development Team may use a planning method that requires them to guesstimate how many Items will fit into a Sprint, and this requires the ability to estimate the effort it will take to get an Item to "Done". The actual effort it will take is intrinsically unknowable because it is affected by the (as yet unknown) impediments the Team will discover as they do the work.

And, as we have seen throughout, the final sentence of the previous paragraph is based on the notion that a Sprint is about delivery, and not feedback. Consequently, it should more properly read: "The purpose of each Sprint is to produce a "Done" Increment to Review."

Development Teams deliver an Increment of product functionality every Sprint. This Increment is useable, so a

Product Owner may choose to immediately release it. If the definition of "Done" for an increment is part of the conventions, standards or guidelines of the development organization, all Scrum Teams must follow it as a minimum.

If "Done" for an increment is not a convention of the development organization, the Development Team of the Scrum Team must define a definition of "Done" appropriate for the product. If there are multiple Scrum Teams working on the system or product release, the Development Teams on all the Scrum Teams must mutually define the definition of "Done."

Annotation 62: Everyone needs to use same definition of "Done"

This is simply saying that there must be a definition of "Done" for each Product, and that everyone working on the same Product should use it. This is really important, as we need to be able to trust each other's' work.

Each Increment is additive to all prior Increments and thoroughly tested, ensuring that all Increments work together.

As Scrum Teams mature, it is expected that their definitions of "Done" will expand to include more stringent criteria for higher quality. New definitions, as used, may uncover work to be done in previously "Done" increments. Any one product or system should have a definition of "Done" that is a standard for any work done on it.

Annotation 63: Quality is part of "Done"

This paragraph states what we've suspected all along, that criteria for quality are part of the definition of "Done".

End Note

Scrum is free and offered in this Guide. Scrum's roles, events, artifacts, and rules are immutable and although implementing only parts of Scrum is possible, the result is not Scrum. Scrum exists only in its entirety and functions well as a container for other techniques, methodologies, and practices.

Annotation 64: Scrum never changes, except when it does...

This End Note has appeared in the previous five (5) version of the Scrum Guide, since the one of July 2011, even as the guide has been mutating. Sorry, we couldn't help it... Dan & Doug ;-)

Acknowledgements

People

Of the thousands of people who have contributed to Scrum, we should single out those who were instrumental at the start: Jeff Sutherland worked with Jeff McKenna and John Scumniotales, and Ken Schwaber worked with Mike Smith and Chris Martin, and all of them worked together. Many others contributed in the ensuing years and without their help Scrum would not be refined as it is today.

History

Ken Schwaber and Jeff Sutherland worked on Scrum until 1995, when they co-presented Scrum at the OOPSLA Conference in 1995. This presentation essentially documented the learning that Ken and Jeff gained over the previous few years, and made public the first formal definition of Scrum.

The history of Scrum is described elsewhere. To honor the first places where it was tried and refined, we recognize Individual, Inc., Newspage, Fidelity Investments, and IDX (now GE Medical).

The Scrum Guide documents Scrum as developed, evolved, and sustained for 20-plus years by Jeff Sutherland and Ken Schwaber. Other sources provide you with patterns, processes, and insights that complement the Scrum framework. These may increase productivity, value, creativity, and satisfaction with the results.

Scrum Dictionary

Scrum uses many terms that are confusing, so we present this Dictionary, which contains terms that are found in the Scrum Guide, the Analysis, the Handbooks, and other sources. It is not a comprehensive list, but it's a start.

Abnormal Termination | A stopping of the Sprint by the Scrum Master at the behest of the Team. This is a 'self-organization thing' and is often threatened but seldom invoked – it is usually used by the Team as a way of saying *'you didn't play nice, so we are going on strike.' (see Self-Organized)*

Acceptance-Based Story | A Story whose Acceptance Criteria does not include a Time-Box; the Time an Acceptance-Based Story takes is a byproduct of getting to "Done." *(see Time-Boxed Story, Acceptance Criteria, Standard of Care, "Done")*

Acceptance Criteria | The description of the objective criteria the Team will use to determine whether or not a Story achieves the Value it represents; the part of "Done" that is separate from the Standard of Care and the General Agreements. *(see Time-Boxed Story, Acceptance-Based Story, Standard of Care, General Agreement, "Done")*

Accountable/Accountability | An accountable person is a person who is ultimately answerable for an activity or decision; the accountable person can be *held to account* for the results of the activity or the making of the decision. There can only be one person accountable for any particular activity or decision. A person is *always* accountable for their commitments. *(see Commitment, compare to Responsible)*

Actionable Story | Synonym for **Ready Story**. *(see Ready Story)*

Agile | 1) Having a decision-making turning radius tight enough to deal with complexity; 2) An umbrella term that encompasses a family of processes known for being 'agile' (Scrum, eXtreme Programming (XP), DSDM, Crystal, Feature Driven Development, Agile2, Kanban, and others). *(see agility)*

Agile Actuary | A professional who does qualitative and quantitative analysis to help Business Owners and Product Champions mitigate risk, support decision-making, evaluate options, and produce the Delivery Forecast. *(see Business Owner, Product Champion, Product Ownership, Delivery Forecast)*

Agile Analysis | Any iterative and incremental method or practice that produces Epics and/or Stories for the Backlog.

Agile Coach | A person who helps people improve their 'agile' skills. The skills might be technical or non-technical, and improvements are typically achieved through training and/or mentoring. The Agile Coach often works with the Team Facilitator to: 1) help the Team Members understand, implement, and improve their use of Scrum and agility; and 2) help the Team identify its Kaizen every Sprint. Every Team must have access to an Agile Coach as needed; this usually requires one Agile Coach for every 2-10 Teams, with five being the 'sweet spot'. *(see Scrum Mastering, Team Facilitator, Kaizen, Team Facilitator)*

Agile Improvement | When an Organization improves its agility, the 'Improvement Stories' compete with other work for prioritization. *(see Improvement Story, compare to Agile Transformation,)*

Agile Transformation | An Organization transforms when it makes radical changes that are more than simply improvement; and Organization in transformation has the Transformation as its main goal, any other work is done simply to determine if the transformation is working. *(compare to Agile Improvement)*

agility | The act of adapting to, and exploiting, the realities we see, as opposed to being predictive or plan-driven. Agility has two primary facets: Physical Agility and Mental Agility. *(see Physical Agility, Mental Agility)*

Agreement-Based Planning | An alternative to Capacity-Driven methods for Sprint Planning. With Agreement-Based Planning Product Ownership and the Team work together to add stories to the Sprint, one at a time, until the Team agrees that the Sprint is 'full'. Things like who is available, technical debt, and the story's definition of "Done", are all taken into account, as they impact what the team can and cannot do. *(see Sprint Planning, compare to Capacity-Driven Planning)*

Alignment | People are in alignment about something when their understandings of the essence of that something are consistent; we often say they "are on the same page". The primary goal of Product Ownership is to have Goals, Strategies, Plans, and Action in alignment from top to bottom – from Stakeholders to Production Team Members. *(note: this concept was originally described by General Helmuth von Moltke (the elder) (1800-1891), and the German term for this concept is "Auftragsklärung")*

Analysis Story | A Story that finds Items or Stories; a Story that conducts Agile Analysis. The most common Analysis Stories find functional Stories by one of various methods (working with SMEs, studying Change Requests, conducting Usability Analysis, etc.); however, there can also be risk analysis Stories (finding risks and fears that need be dealt with), process analysis Stories (finding process improvements), and so on. *(see Agile Analysis, Backlog Refinement)*

Architecturally Significant Story | A Functional Story that causes the Team to make one or more architectural decisions, which is then validated by the fact that there is existing, working functionality using the decisions. *(see Functional Story, Architecture)*

Architecture | The collection of decisions about how a system will be built – from Grady Booch in the early 80's.

Back Burner | Synonym for **Work Backlog.** *(see Work Backlog)*

Backlog | An ordered list of Backlog Items to be worked on. *(see Backlog Item, Product Backlog, Work Backlog, Results Backlog)*

Backlog Item | A single unit of work on the Backlog, an Item is either an Epic or a Story. *(see Backlog, Epic, Story)*

Backlog Maintenance | Synonym for **Backlog Refinement.** *(see Backlog Refinement)*

Backlog Refinement | The act of preparing a Backlog to make it ready for Planning. This includes: extracting Stories from Epics, refining Stories to make them Ready, and ordering the Stories. There could be Refinement Stories, Sessions, or both. Synonyms include Grooming, Backlog Maintenance, and Story Time. *(see Backlog, Planning, Order, Epic, Story, Ready)*

Bug | A simple change that does not require an acceptance test; examples include correcting a misspelling in a dialog box or moving an interface element on the screen. Often used (incorrectly, in my view) as a synonym for Defect. *(see Defect)*

BuildUp | A BuildUp graph is any graph that shows the completion of Backlog as a function of Time.

BurnDown | A BurnDown graph is any graph that shows the amount of remaining Backlog (Items or Tasks) as a function of Time. Many people and tools use BurnDowns, but they have been largely deprecated from Scrum as they are inherently predictive, and not agile.

BurnUp | Synonym for **BuildUp**. *(see BuildUp)*

Business Organization | The organization the Team belongs to, or works for. The Business Organization provides services the Team needs in order to exist, such as Human Resources, Logistics, Facilities, Contracting, Training, and so on. The Business Organization is typically referred to as either "the Business" or "the Organization", depending on context.

Business Owner | A Product Ownership role that represents a person who is accountable to the Business Organization for maximizing the overall value of Deliverable Results, which could represent one, or many, Products. The Business Owner owns the Results Backlog, and is also called the Business's Product Owner. *(see Product*

Ownership, Business Organization, Results Backlog)

Business Value (BV) | A property of an Item that simply indicates that some external Stakeholder wants it; it is very hard to quantify, even though we continue to try to do so.

Business's Product Owner | Synonym for **Business Owner**. *(see Business Owner)*

Cadence | Synonym for **Rhythm**. *(see Rhythm)*

Cancelling a Sprint | The Team's Product Owner (Team Captain) may cancel a Sprint at any time, usually because the Business Owner's objective for the Sprint isn't going to be met or because the objective is no longer what is needed.

Capability | A Story that provides value to an external Stakeholder; an Item that has Business Value. *(see Story, compare to Chore)*

Capacity | An estimate or prediction of the rate that a Team or Organization *will be able* to develop Product; it is often used in Release Planning. Often confused with Velocity and WorkRate. *(see Velocity, WorkRate)*

Capacity-Driven Planning – Any planning method based on an assumption of future Capacity. *(see Capacity, compare to Agreement-Based Planning)*

'Catch' Feedback | Feedback obtained by actively listening to responses from a stakeholder during review of an artifact (such as a completed story or product increment). *(see 'Pull' Feedback)*

Change Agent | A person who helps the Organization adopt, implement, and sustain Scrum, and understand how best to support and work with Scrum Teams – this includes organizational design. There needs to be at least one Change Agent per Organization. The Change Agent is usually also an Agile Coach (with expertise in organizational behavior), and is considered the 'senior Scrum Master' in the Organization. *(see Scrum Mastering, Agile Coach)*

Chief Scrum Master (CSM) | The Team Captain of a Scrum Master

Team; we expect to see a CSM for every Pod, sub-Pod, Group and sub-Group. *(see Team Captain, Scrum Master, Scrum Master Team, Pod, Group)*

Chore | A Story that provides value to the Team or Product, as opposed to an external Stakeholder; an Item whose value is other than Business Value. *(see Story, compare to Capability)*

Clean Code | 1) Code that is easy to change: that is extensible, modifiable, and maintainable. 2) Code that has little or no Technical Debt. *(see Technical Debt)*

CleanUp Story | A Story that *apologizes* to the Code Base about something bad that happened, and *promises* to fix it. It usually documents what is wrong and indicates what needs to be accomplished to fix it. A Cleanup Story is a story that tells us where the mess is and what we have to do to clean it up.

Clients | The people who will be using, consuming, or working with the Product/Results the Team is developing.

Co-Located | A Team 'being co-located' means that its Team Members must be close enough together (either physically or virtually) that they can talk to each other within seconds or minutes, rather than hours or days.

Code Complete | A Product Increment is code complete when the development team agrees that no entirely new source code (including automated tests) needs to be added.

Coding Story | A Story that has Code as its primary result.

Commitment | 1) One of the least understood of the Scrum Values; the Team commits to living their Values and doing their due diligence to get Stories "Done;" 2) an obligation a person has promised to accomplish, 3) often used as a synonym for Sprint Commitment. *(see Scrum Values, "Done", Sprint Commitment)*

Complex Problem | Any problem that is too complicated for any one person to fully grok (understand fully).

Conflict Resolution Process | A process that resolves issues resulting from disagreements, disputes, violations of Team Norms or Values, and so on. A Conflict Resolution Process should: 1) be fair and legal; 2) have an escalating series of steps (negotiations, agreements, discussions, sanctions, punishments, etc.) that 3) ultimately lead to removal from the Team, expulsion from the Organization, or worse. *(see Team Norms, Team Values)*

'Continuous Development' Strategy | A development strategy for a Sprint where the Backlog represents a Continuous Flow of work for the Team, and the Sprint simply defines the duration until 'inspecting and adapting' the "Done" Results. *(compare to 'Small Project' Strategy)*

Continuous Flow | 1) Moving products through a production system without separating them into lots; 2) In Scrum, doing all work on an as-needed, just-in-time, basis, with each chunk of work being completed without interruptions. The work the Scrum Team does every day includes the Daily Scrum, Production, Maintaining the Results Backlog, and Backlog Refinement.

Continuous Planning | Just-in-Time planning that supports the 'Continuous Development' Strategy by providing the agility required to meet the needs of a chaotic requirements environment. The Team Captain's decision-making inherent in Continuous Planning is often informed by GOs that were provided by a Business Owner. *(see Planning, 'Continuous Development' Strategy, Team Captain, GO, Business Owner)*

Coordinator | In a Team Swarm, the Coordinator is the Team Member who is 'in charge' of the Story being worked on. *(see Team Swarm, Stay-At-Home, Swarmer)*

Courage | Team Members must have the courage to make reality visible, do the right thing, and work on tough problems. *(see Scrum Values)*

Crew Chief | A journeyman who directs work at a work site; this term is used to refer to a **Team Captain** when the Team Captain is clearly also a member of the DevTeam and is Scrum Mastering. *(see Team Captain, DevTeam, Scrum Mastering)*

Cross-Cutting Workgroup | In a **Team-of-Teams**, a Cross-Cutting Workgroup is a Virtual Scrum Team, consisting of Team Members from multiple Teams, that has a specific mission or problem to solve. *(see Team-of-Teams, Virtual Team)*

Cross-Functional | Synonym for **Self-Contained**. *(see Self-Contained)*

CSM | Acronym for **Chief Scrum Master**. *(see Chief Scrum Master)*

CURB | An acronym that stands for Complex, Unknown, Risky or Big. CURB is a mnemonic to help you remember how to determine if a functional Story is actually an Epic. *(see Epic)*

Customers | The people who will be paying for the Product, or Results.

Daily Scrum | Scrum's daily 'inspect and adapt' ceremony; its purpose is to collect 'today's reality', compare it to the Sprint's Backlog, Goal, Objective, and Kaizen, and 'inspect and adapt' to determine what to do today. *(see Kaizen, Sprint Backlog, Sprint Goal, Sprint Objective)*

Daily Standup | Synonym for **Daily Scrum.** *(see Daily Scrum)*

Defect | 1) Anything about a Product that is seen as 'wrong' by a Stakeholder; defects usually result in a new Item being added to the Backlog; 2) A bug, failure, flaw or error in an application or program that results in unexpected, incorrect or unintended ways. *(see Bug)*

Definition of "Done" (DoD) | 1) Synonym for **"Done"**; 2) often used erroneously as a synonym for **Standard of Care**. *(see "Done", Standard of Care)*

Definition of Ready (DoR) | Synonym for **Ready.** *(see Ready Story)*

Deliverable Results | Scrum Teams and Organizations produce Deliverable Results for Stakeholders iteratively and incrementally; these Deliverable Results are often called Product. *(see Product, Increment)*

Delivery Forecast | The Delivery Forecast is 'owned' by the Product Champion, and predicts Scope, Delivery Dates, and Costs. It should be based on Data, not Hope. It is important to note that the Team saying they will deliver on time is not Data, and telling the Team what it will deliver, and when, is not Data. *(see Product Champion)*

Developer | Synonym for **Team Member**. *(see Team Member)*

Development Team | The subset of the Scrum Team that is actually producing Results; this may, or may not, include the Scrum Team's Captain and Facilitator. *(see Scrum Team, Team Captain, Team Facilitator)*

DevTeam | Synonym for **Development Team**. *(see Development Team)*

Do Work | Every day during the Sprint, the Team is said to "Do Work", which includes: 1) The Team Swarms with its Subject Matter Experts in order to get Stories that are 'In Progress' to "Done"; 2) As Stories get to "Done", the Team Captain determines which Ready Stories should be moved from the Work Backlog to become Work In Progress; 3) The Team makes progress on its Kaizen; and 4) The Team discusses and removes Impediments. *(see Subject Matter Expert, Team Captain, Ready Story, Work Backlog, Work in Progress, Kaizen, Impediment)*

DoD | 1) Acronym for **Definition of "Done"**; 2) often used as a synonym for **Standard of Care**. *(see "Done", Standard of Care)*

"Done" | 1) A piece of work is "Done" when it satisfies the (pre-existing) agreement between Stakeholders and Developers about what it takes for the work to be complete; 2) "Done" for a Story usually consists of Acceptance Criteria (which could include a TimeBox), a Standard of Care, and General Agreements; 3) A Software Increment is "Done" when *"the increment consists of thoroughly tested, well-structured, and well-written code that has been built into an executable and that the user operation of the functionality is documented… This is the definition of a "Done" increment."* (per Ken Schwaber, *Agile Project Management with Scrum*, Microsoft Press, 2004, pg. 12). The concept of "Done" has often been extended to Epics, Sprints, Releases, and so on… *(see Acceptance-Based Story, Time-Boxed Story, Acceptance Criteria, Standard of Care, General Agreement, compare to UnDone)*

Doneness Agreement | Synonym for **Story Agreement**. *(see Story Agreement)*

Due Diligence | A person, Team, or Organization is doing its 'due diligence' when it is taking necessary steps to avoid harm to people or property.

Effort [for a Story] | The amount of time it actually took to complete a Story (get the Story to "Done"), and is usually measured in Hours or PersonDays. *(see "Done", compare to Size [of a Story])*

EffortPoint | A relative measure of the actual effort it will take to 'do' a Story. Often confused with StoryPoint. *(see StoryPoint, Ideal Engineering Hour/Day)*

Empirical Process | An empirical process is a process based on empiricism, which asserts that knowledge comes from experience and decisions are made based on what is known. *(synonym for agility)*

Environmental Variables | Factors affecting Effort that are not related to the actual Story. These include, but are not limited to, Technical Debt, Organizational Noise, SME Availability, and Team Ability. *(see Technical Debt, Organizational Noise, SME Availability, Team Ability)*

Epic | 1) a Backlog Item that is too Complex, Unknown, Risky, or Big (CURB) for the Team to agree to do all at once; 2) a named Container of other Epics and Stories. *(see CURB)*

Estimation Game | Any of a variety of consensus-based methods of estimating.

Executive Review | A Review for the business to discuss project, process, or people issues. This is not a part of Scrum, but is often necessary for legitimate business reasons. *(see Project Review, Sprint Review, Product Review, Progress Review)*

Exemplar Story | An example Item used as a reference point for Estimation. For example, we could have exemplar Small, Medium, and Large Stories as reference points for Estimating Story Size or

Effort. *(see Effort [for a Story], Size [of a Story])*

Extracting Stories | The Team does Backlog Refinement with its Subject Matter Experts and/or Product Champions, its Business Owner, and its Stakeholders to assure that there are Ready Stories in the Work Backlog. This includes Extracting Stories from the Results Backlog to the Work Backlog. *(see Backlog Refinement)*

eXtreme Programming (XP) | An agile development process whose practices largely focus on the production of Clean Code. *(see Clean Code)*

Feature | Something a software product enables a user to do. *(see Capability)*

Feature Complete | A state of software indicating that no more features need to be added.

Flow Management Team | Synonym for **Pod Flow Management Team** *(see Pod Management Team)*

Focus | Everything the Team does must have a focus, and the Team Members must focus on what is important in everything they do. *(see Scrum Values)*

Forecast | Short for **Sprint Forecast.** *(See Sprint Forecast)*

Freezer | The portion of the Backlog that contains Items that are 'out of scope.'

Fridge | Synonym for **Results Backlog.** *(see Results Backlog)*

Front Burner | The portion of the Backlog that the Team has agreed to work on 'now'. Depending on your 'flavor' or Scrum, this can either be the Sprint Backlog or the Work in Progress (WIP). *(see Sprint Backlog, Work in Progress)*

Full-Time | Each Team Member is full-time; he or she *belongs* to a single Team. However, the Team, because it is self-organized, may 'loan out' one or more of its Team Members to work elsewhere on Virtual Teams or as a Subject Matter Experts. *(see Virtual Team, Subject Matter Expert)*

Functional Story | A Story that produces working code that has actual, demonstrable user value. A Functional Story's Acceptance Criteria usually consists of a single Acceptance Test, and verifying that the Test passes is part of the Story itself.

General Agreements | The Part of a Story's definition of "Done" that contains information about which SMEs will be involved, who will be the Story Coordinator, what is 'out of scope' for the Story, and so on. *(see "Done")*

GO | acronym for **Guidance and Objectives**. GOs are typically developed by Business Owners to help Team Captains and Product Champions with their decision-making. *(see Guidance, Objective, Business Owner, Team Captain, Product Champion)*

Gold-Plating | 1) The incorporation of costly and unnecessary features or refinements into a product or structure; 2) making changes to a to a well-defined unit of work that are outside of the original agreed-upon scope. *(see Acceptance Criteria)*

Governance | An Organization's Governance Mechanism is the method it uses to manage and make decisions.

Grooming | Synonym for **Backlog Refinement.** *(see Backlog Refinement)*

Group | A Group is a collection of Pods and sub-Groups along with a Group Leadership Team. *(see Pod, Group Leadership Team)*

Group Leadership Team | A Virtual Scrum Team that consists of the Group Owner (as its Team Captain) and its subordinate Pod and sub-Group Owners. *(see Virtual Team, Team Captain, Group Owner, Pod Owner)*

Group Owner | A Business Owner who is accountable for maximizing the Value produced by a Group; the Group Owner is the Team Captain of the Group Leadership Team. *(see Group, Team Captain, Group Leadership Team)*

Guidance | Advice or information, given by someone in authority, aimed at helping other people achieve objectives or resolve problems. *(see Accountable, GO, Objective)*

Hardening Sprint | A Hardening Sprint is a specialized sprint dedicated to stabilizing the code base so that it is robust enough for release; it is often necessary because the Team failed to use an appropriate Standard of Care when it did its work. Using a Hardening Sprint is not recommended, and the need for it should be eliminated by improving engineering practice. If the need for hardening exists, it should be accomplished a little at a time by using Cleanup Stories within Sprints, not by dedicating a complete Sprint to hardening.

High-Ceremony Agility | Any Agile process that has many meeting, artifacts, or practices.

Humor | Everyone needs a sense of humor; if we can't laugh at some of the things we do, we'd have to cry. *(see Team Values)*

Hybridized Agile | An approach to creating a better breed of agile by combining various agile and existing processes; this often leads to Paradigm Induced Blindness. *(see Paradigm Induced Blindness)*

Ideal Effort | The amount of effort it would take to build something if conditions were as they *should* be; there are no impediments of any kind, and you don't require any magic or miracles. This is actually a measure of Size because Ideal Effort would not differ from Team to Team. *(see Ideal Engineering Hour/ Day, Impediment)*

Ideal Engineering Hour/Day | An estimate of actual effort that ignores disruptions or disasters; an Ideal Hour/Day is an Hour/Day that has no interruptions, but does not 'wish away' other Impediments. *(see Ideal Effort, Impediment)*

Impediment | Anything that is causing the Team to not be at its best. These could be fears, risks, or problems.

Improvement Backlog | A Backlog of Improvement Stories; the Improvement Backlog is usually created and 'owned' by a Scrum Master Team. *(see Improvement Story, Scrum Master Team)*

Improvement Story | A Story whose goal is to improve an

Organization's or Team's agility. *(see Story, Improvement Backlog)*

Improvement Team | another term for Pod/Group Scrum Master Team. The Improvement Team creates and manages the Pod/Group's Improvement Backlog. *(see Improvement Backlog)*

InBox | Items in the Backlog that have not yet been prioritized.

Increment | The Team completes each Story, it continuously produces Results (proposed and partial Deliverables) that require Stakeholder feedback. These Results are accumulated to product a Product Increment, and the Increment should always be "Done" and in reviewable condition. *(see Product)*

Informed Process | An informed process is one in which decision-making is informed by gathering observations in progressive steps. *(synonym for Agile Process)*

Interested Bystander | People who think that they are Stakeholders, but actually 'don't matter' to you, are called Interested Bystanders.

Intraspective | A discussion by the Scrum Team about its Practices or Teamwork that occurs *within* the Sprint: it is often precipitated by an event that 'didn't go well.' *(compare to Retrospective)*

Intrinsic Difficulty | The Intrinsic Difficulty of a Story is inherent in the Acceptance Criteria, and, for a Functional Story, is based on the complexity involved in the design activities themselves and the complexity of the resulting designs and algorithms. *(see Size [of a Story], Functional Story)*

Item | Short for **Backlog Item**, synonym for **Story**. *(see Backlog Item, Story)*

Kaizen | 1) A philosophy of continuous improvement of working practices, personal efficiency, etc, and 2) a single improvement for a person, Team, or Organization.

Kanban Method | A method of organizing and managing the work for delivering services to customers. The main strength of Kanban (from a Scrum point of view) is that its Planning is continuous, which makes it more likely to keep up with reality, and hence more agile.

Kanban Values | The Kanban Values are: Respect, Values, Focus, Transparency, Understanding, Leadership, Agreement, Collaboration, and Flow. *(see Values)*

Kanban(ish) Variant | The Kanban(ish) Variant of Scrum is one in which the standard (batch) Sprint Planning is replaced by continuous Planning throughout the Sprint. Scrum$_H$ is a Kanban(ish) variant of Scrum. *(see Scrum$_H$)*

Leadership | 1) The act of being followed, 2) The interplay between decision-making and team direction.

Leadership Team | synonym for **Group Leadership Team**. *(see Group Leadership Team)*

Lean Principles | Lean Principles focus on creating value while eliminating waste, thus making a Value Stream (process flow) more efficient. Two of the Lean Principles that are built into *good* implementations of Scrum are 'Pull, don't Push' and 'Minimize Inventory.'

Lollygagging | To waste time aimlessly, to waste an excessive amount of time. Note: the 'right' amount of time is called Slack. *(see Slack)*

Management Team | Synonym for **Pod Flow Management Team** *(see Pod Flow Management Team)*

Mental Agility | Having situational awareness and using feedback to make the decisions necessary to be agile. *(see agility, Physical Agility)*

Mission | A short statement of why the Team exists – what it does, for whom, and why – the Mission is often obvious from looking at the Team's name.

Mission Protection | Ongoing, public commitment from the Business Organization to safeguard the Scrum Team's ability to achieve their Mission. *(see Mission, Business Organization)*

Modern Scrum | Any Scrum that is consistent with the definition of the *Scrum Guide*. *(see Scrum Guide)*

MTS | Acronym for **Multi-Team Scrum**. *(see Multi-Team Scrum)*

Multi-Team Scrum | A type of Scaled Scrum that involves Teams-of-Teams, and is documented in the *Scrum Handbook: Multi-Team Scrum (MTS)*. *(see Team-of-Teams)*

Objective | A thing aimed at or sought; something that is wanted, but not guaranteed or committed to. *(see GO)*

One Big Thing (OBT) | In any model, any entity in the model should be defined by 'One Big Thing'; its reason for being. If you can't find the One Big Thing for any given entity, then either the model is defective, or you don't understand the model.

Openness | There should be no secrets between/amongst Team Members about things relevant to the work and their ability to do the work; this requires some measure of Psychological Safety. *(see Scrum Values, Psychological Safety)*

Order | Refers to the order of a Backlog; the order that the appropriate Product Owner wants the Items worked on. *(see Priority)*

Organizational Noise | An Organization that empowers and nurtures its Teams is said to be a 'quiet' Organization, while one with many procedures, meetings, interruptions, and the like, is said to be 'noisy.' *(see Environmental Variables)*

Pairing | Pairing is a Swarming Pattern often associated with eXtreme Programming (XP), is when each Story is worked on by two Developers, working side-by-side at one computer, collaborating on the same design, algorithm, code or test. Many Teams have found it useful to rotate Pairs every 1-2 hours, which is referred to as Polygamous Pairing. *(see Team Swarm)*

Paradigm Induced Blindness | When a person follows a process 'blindly' because the process is so convoluted it just overloads the person's head.

Physical Agility | A Team, Project, or Organization has Physical Agility if its processes provide opportunities to obtain the feedback necessary to enable agility. *(see agility, Mental Agility)*

PlaceHolder Story | A PlaceHolder Story is a Story that represents a 'known unknown' (or contains resources to be used for 'known unknowns'). One of the most common issues for Scrum Teams is what to do about work that it expects to have to do during a Sprint, but doesn't actually know the details about yet, such as fixing bugs in existing systems, or expected sales support efforts. Using PlaceHolder Stories is a form of buffer and is used as part of contingency planning.

Plan of Action | A tentative plan, developed by the Team, of how the Sprint might be carried out. The purpose of the Plan of Action is not to have a plan, *per se*, but to enable the Team to justify to itself that doing the work is possible. *(see Sprint Planning)*

Planning | A session with the whole Scrum Team (including the Team Captain) to decide which Stories should be "Done" next. *(see Sprint Planning, Team Captain, "Done")*

Planning Day | Planning day takes place 'between' Sprints, and includes the Sprint Review (broken into the Product and Progress Reviews when necessary), the Retrospective, and Sprint Planning for the next Sprint.

Pod | A Pod is a Team-of-Teams consisting of Production Teams, sub-Pods, a Pod Management Team, and other (physical and virtual) Teams, that produces similar Products for similar Product Champions. *(see Product Champion, Pod Management Team, Team-of-Teams, Production Team)*

Pod Flow Management Team | A Virtual Scrum Team that has the Pod Owner as its Team Captain, and its (immediate) subordinate Team Captains, Product Champions, and sub-Pod Owners as Team Members. The Pod Management Team manages the flow of work within the Pod. *(see Virtual Team, Team Captain, Product Champion, Pod Owner)*

Pod Owner | A Business Owner who is accountable for maximizing the Value of the Results produced by a Pod; the Pod Owner is the

Team Captain of the Pod Flow Management Team. *(see Pod, Team Captain, Business Owner, Pod Management Team)*

Potentially Releasable | Synonym for **"Done"**. *(See "Done")*

Potentially Shippable | Synonym for **"Done"**. *(See "Done")*

Priority | The priority of an Item is based on how important it is. Normally, the importance of an Item would be based on its Business Value, but in Scrum, an Item's priority is determined by when it will be undertaken (where it is in the Backlog), not by how valuable it is. *(see Order)*

Product | 1) (in Scrum) Something that a Team or Organization produces for delivery to its Stakeholders; a Product consists of Deliverable Results; 2) (in popular use) A specific marketable/ sellable/usable unit, such as 'website ABC' or the '123 Counting Program.' *(see Deliverable Results, Team-Product, Product-Product)*

Product Backlog | A Product Backlog is an ordered list of everything that is known to be needed in a Product. This term is usually used when the Product is actually a Product-Product. When the Product is a Team-Product, its Product backlog is imbedded in the Team's Work Backlog. *(see Product-Product, Team-Product, Work Backlog)*

Product Backlog Item | Synonym for **Backlog Item** *(see Backlog Item)*

Product Champion | A Product Ownership role that represents the interests of a cohesive set of Stakeholders focused on the same Product. The Product Champion is a Business Owner who is restricted to a single Product, represents that Product's Backlog, owns the Product Vision, and provides/ identifies Subject Matter Experts to the Organization to aid in development and reviews of that Product. Also called the Product's Product Owner. *(see Product, Product Ownership, Business Owner, Product Backlog, Product-Product Owner)*

Product Increment | Synonym for **Increment** *(see Increment)*

Product Owner | Depending on who you are talking to, the term 'Product Owner' could refer to any (or all) of the primary Product

Ownership roles (Team Captain, Product Champion, Business Owner), but usually refers to a Product Champion. *(see Product Ownership, Product Champion, Team Captain, Business Owner)*

Product Owner Team | A Virtual Team made up of Product Owners (and others) that provide guidance to Organizations consisting of a Team-of-Teams *(see Virtual Team, Team-of-Teams, Leadership Team, Flow Management Team)*

Product Ownership | The collection of Responsibilities and Accountabilities that sit between the Stakeholders and the Developers; these responsibilities range from creating a strategic vision to delivery management to determining what work will be worked on next. *(see Team Captain, Business Owner, Product Champion, Agile Actuary)*

Product-Product | A Product that an Organization delivers to its Stakeholders; it has an associated Product Backlog and Product Champion. In some circles, a Product-Product is referred to as a 'Real' Product, as opposed to a Team's Product. *(see Product Backlog, Product Champion, 'Team-Product)*

Product-Product Owner | Synonym for **Product Champion**. *(see Product Champion)*

Product Review | A Team session at the end of a Sprint where the Team (along with its Product Ownership and Stakeholders) reviews their Increment in order to get feedback on what to do next, what to do better, and so on. *(see Increment, Product Ownership, Sprint Review, Progress Review)*

Product Vision | The Product Vision is a quick summary expressing how the product supports the Organization and/or Stakeholders.

Product's Product Owner | Synonym for **Product Champion**. *(see Product Champion)*

Production Team | A Scrum Team that *develops Product* to be used by Customers, Clients, and the like.

Progress Review | A meeting including Product Ownership and

Customers about 'how the work is going'. Its purpose is to gather information and set expectations with the Customers. *(See Executive Review, Sprint Review, Product Review, Project Review)*

Project Review | Another name for **Progress Review** when the work is organized into a Project and, therefore, has a Delivery Forecast (Project Plan). *(see Progress Review, Delivery Forecast)*

Psychological Safety | the belief that one will not be punished or humiliated for speaking up with ideas, questions, concerns, or mistakes. *(see Openness)*

'Pull' Feedback | Feedback obtained by actively engaging a stakeholder during review of any product artifact (completed story or product increment). *(see 'Catch' Feedback)*

Quality Code | Synonym for **Clean Code** *(see Clean Code)*

Ready | A Ready Story is small, well-defined, and ready to take to Planning. Generally, this means that the Story's definition of "Done" is a '10 minute discussion' away from being agreed to. *(see Well-Defined Story)*

'Real' Product | Synonym for **Product-Product**. *(see Product-Product)*

Refactoring | Rewriting existing source code in order to improve its readability, reusability or structure without affecting its meaning or behavior.

Refinement | Synonym for **Backlog Refinement.** *(see Backlog Refinement)*

Regular Sync-Up | A re-plan/plan the Team has on a regular basis (typically daily) in order to collect together an understanding of 'changes in reality' in order to deal with it. *(see Daily Scrum)*

Regulators | Stakeholders, either inside or outside your Business Organization, who can regulate, or constrain, the Product/Results the Team is producing and/or the process that the Team uses. Examples include things like Cyber Security, CISA, ITAR Compliance, SOX, Medical, etc. *(see Stakeholder)*

Regulatory Constraint | An official standard, rule, or regulation that can affect either what is built (e.g., it must be bi-lingual), how it is built (e.g., the Code must be completely protected by Tests), or both. *(see Regulators)*

Release | A movement of the Team's Deliverable Results from the development environment to some other environment, for some other reason than development. Examples include alpha releases, beta releases, go-live releases, releases to a test lab, and so on. Releases are not a part of Scrum; releasing product must be done with Stories – there is no 'release' ceremony in Scrum.

Release Sprint | A specialized Sprint whose purpose is to Release Deliverable Results; it contains Stories specific to Release Activities and finishing UnDone Work. A Release Sprint usually contains no additional development. *(see UnDone)*

Release Strategy | A term used to refer to all types of Release Planning, Release Monitoring, and the like. It is not a part of Scrum, but a Release Strategy is often needed with Scrum – in part to decide what work will be left UnDone until the Release Sprint.

Representative | Synonym for **Team Representative**. *(see Team Representative)*

Resolution Process | Short for **Conflict Resolution Process**. *(see Conflict Resolution Process)*

Respect | Respect is the belief that people are always doing the best they can do at any given moment. *(see Scrum Values)*

Responsible | Responsible people are the individual(s) who actually do the work; responsibility can be shared. The degree of responsibility is determined by the person with the "Accountability"; and Responsibility is often confused with Accountability. *(see Accountable)*

Results | Short for **Deliverable Results.** *(see Deliverable Results)*

Results Backlog | A prioritized list of Deliverable Results that a Business Owner hopes to deliver to Stakeholders. The Stakeholders and Business Owner maintain the Results Backlog by adding new

Deliverables and prioritizing/re-prioritizing. *(see Business Owner)*

Retrospective | Short for **Team Retrospective.** *(see Team Retrospective)*

Review | Short for **Sprint Review.** *(see Sprint Review)*

Rhythm | Movement or procedure with uniform or patterned recurrence. Scrum has two primary Rhythms: the Daily rhythm of work, and the Sprintly rhythm of feedback and planning.

Safety | Short for **Psychological Safety**. *(see Psychological Safety)*

Scale-Ready | A single-team process or practice is said to be 'scale-ready' when it can be easily applied or extended to an organization of many teams.

Scaling | The changes in Structure and Governance that enable successful growth (or reduction) of production. In general, the increase or decrease in one or more dimensions of an organization in order to improve success.

Scaling Scrum with Scrum® (SSwS) | A Scaling method that leverages what we already know about Scrum rather than developing new concepts. SSWS is the basis for Multi-Team Scrum. *(See Multi-Team Scrum)*

Scenario | An interaction with the System that consists of a single thread, and is represented by a single Acceptance Test. *(see Use Case)*

Scrum | An agile framework, model, or philosophy for Product Development, *not* Project Management. There have been, are, and will be, many variants of Scrum; it is more of a concept than a prescription.

Scrum$_P$ | Scrum$_P$ is a variant of Scrum in which the Product Owner 'lives with' the Stakeholders and is their representative to the Team. In Scrum$_P$ the Product Owner may not change priorities during the Sprint. Scrum$_P$ is defined by the Scrum Primer at scrumprimer.org, and the "P" in Scrum$_P$ stands for "Primer".

Scrum$_G$ | Scrum$_G$ is a variant of Scrum in which the Product Owner is a member of the Team who consults with the Stakeholders. In Scrum$_G$ the Team's Product Owner may work with the Team to change priorities during the Sprint. Scrum$_G$ is defined by the Scrum Guide at scrumguides.org, and the "G" in Scrum$_G$ stands for "Guide".

Scrum$_H$ | Scrum$_H$ is a variant of Scrum in which Product Ownership is shared between a Team Captain on the Team and Business Owners and Product Champions outside the Team. Scrum$_H$ is described in *The Scrum Handbook: Single-Team Scrum*, and the "H" in Scrum$_H$ stands for "Handbook."

Scrum-of-Scrums (SoS) | In a multi-scrum-team environment: 1) a meeting held after all the individual Scrum Teams' Daily Scrums, consisting of a representative/ambassador from each Scrum Team, in order to achieve cross-team collaboration; 2) a virtual Scrum Team composed of the Scrum Masters from each Scrum Team; and 3) any virtual Scrum Team composed of representatives from various Scrum Teams.

Scrum Board | Synonym for **Story Board**. *(see Story Board)*

Scrum Guide | Any of *The Scrum Guides* published by Schwaber and Sutherland at scrumguides.org; Scrum Guides are usually distinguished by their publication date, like *The 2017 Scrum Guide*.

Scrum Master | Depending on who you are talking to, the term 'Scrum Master' could refer to somebody playing any (or all) of the Scrum Mastering roles (Team Facilitator, Change Agent, Team Coach), but usually refers to the Team Facilitator. *(see Scrum Mastering, Team Facilitator, Change Agent, Team Coach)*

Scrum Master Community | The collection of people doing Scrum Mastering within an Organization; this includes Team Facilitators. Agile Coaches, and Change Agents. This group is responsible for 'making Scrum better' within the Organization. They have an Improvement Backlog (often virtual or invisible) of changes they would like to have in the Organization to make it more amenable to Scrum. *(see Scrum Mastering, Team Facilitator, Agile Coach, Change Agent)*

Scrum Master Team | The Scrum Master Team for a Pod or Group is a Virtual Scrum Team consisting of all the Scrum Masters of the subordinate Teams, Pods, and Groups; with the Scrum Master of the Ldrsp/Mgmt Team as its Team Captain. *(see Virtual Team, Pod, Group, Management Team, Leadership Team)*

Scrum Mastering | Enabling, Empowering, and improving People, Teams, and Organizations in order to allow them to do their jobs better. People playing Scrum Master roles apply Servant Leadership principles to teamwork and practices in order to facilitate (making an action or process easy or easier) them becoming more effective and enjoyable. *(see Team Facilitator, Agile Coach, Change Agent)*

Scrum Team | A Scrum Team (commonly called the "Team") is a small, co-located, self-organized, self-contained, value-driven, group of full-time Team Members who are organized around a Mission. Their job is to produce High-Quality Results at a Sustainable Pace.

Scrum Values | The Scrum Values are: Openness, Focus, Commitment, Respect, and Courage. *(see Values)*

Self-Contained | A self-contained (also called Cross-Functional) team is one that contains all the knowledge and skills necessary to accomplish its objectives and goals: in software development this means that there are people who can test, there are people who can code, there are people who do analysis, there are people who write documentation, and so on.

Self-Organized | A self-organized team is one that chooses how best to accomplish its work, rather than being directed (micro-managed) by others outside the team. *(see Tactical Agility)*

Single Item Flow | Single item flow (also called 'single piece flow' or 'one piece flow') is a lean manufacturing concept that says that each individual Item will move through the manufacturing process *all at once* with no waiting between steps. On Scrum Teams, this means Stories don't wait for people who have skills they need – the people are available when they're needed. *(see Team Swarm)*

Single-Team Scrum (STS) | The Scrum that is described in the *Scrum Handbook: Single-Team Scrum (STS).*

Size [of a Story] | A measure of 'how much' Product was (or will be) produced by the Story. The Size of a Functional Story is typically based on the Story's Intrinsic Difficulty, Ideal Effort, number of 'moving parts', or some such. *(see Intrinsic Difficulty, Ideal Effort, compare to Effort [for a Story])*

Slack | Time people use to think, innovate, and improve themselves, the right amount of time to 'waste' (from Tom DeMarco), *(see lollygagging)*

Small [size of a Team] | A Team needs to be small enough to have one (or a few conversations) at the same time, so that everybody can be 'on the same page' all (or most of) the time. A Team must be small enough to remain nimble and be large enough to complete significant work in a Sprint. Typically, this means that a Team has between three and nine Members – the 'sweet spot' for software development seems to be about five.

'Small Project' Strategy | A development strategy that treats a Sprint as a Small Project, with a forecasted, anticipated, Result. *(compare to 'Continuous Development' Strategy)*

SME | Acronym for **Subject Matter Expert.** *(see Subject Matter Expert)*

SME Availability | An Environmental Variable that indicates whether or not there are Subject Matter Experts available who have the knowledge or expertise you need, when you need it. *(see Environmental Variables)*

SoC | Acronym for **Standard of Care.** *(see Standard of Care)*

Spike | An XP (eXtreme Programming) term that describes Stories that figure out answers to tough technical or design problems. Spikes address only the problem under consideration and ignore all other concerns. Most Spikes get thrown away, which differentiates them from Architecturally Significant Stories. *(see Architecturally Significant Story)*

Sprint | A fixed period of time (less than a month) in which a Team produces an Increment for review. The Sprint length is defined by the interval between Product Reviews, is usually consistent across Sprints, and must not be changed once the Sprint has started. *(see Increment)*

Sprint Backlog | A 'living document' that consists of the Stories the Team has brought into the Sprint, along with their definitions of "Done" and (possibly) Tasks. *(see Work in Progress, Sprint Forecast, "Done", Task)*

Sprint Cancellation | Synonym for **Cancelling a Sprint**. *(see Cancelling a Sprint)*

Sprint Commitment | The Team commits to its Sprint Goal and to doing its due diligence to assure that all completed Stories are actually "Done". *(see Sprint Goal, Sprint Backlog)*

Sprint End | The time when work in the Sprint is ended in order to Review, Retrospect, and Plan. The Sprint End is usually a set date and time, but may be pre-determined by an event, as "We'll have Sprint End when Doug gets back from Europe…" *(see Sprint Planning, Sprint Review, Team Retrospective)*

Sprint Forecast | 1) when using the 'Small Project' Strategy for a Sprint, the Team's anticipated Result for the Sprint; or 2) The Team's best guess about how many Stories, Tasks or Story Points will be accomplished in the Sprint. There is no requirement for a Team to have a Sprint Forecast and, In any case, the Team is not accountable for achieving the Sprint Forecast; it is, at most, a 'best guess' – it is not a plan, commitment, or promise. *(see Accountable, Sprint Goal)*

Sprint Goal | The Sprint Goal is something that the Scrum Team members agree to accomplish *together* within the Sprint. The Sprint Goal defines success for the Sprint, and the Team will do 'whatever it takes' to meet it. Committing to the Sprint Goal, rather than the Sprint Backlog, allows the Team the 'wiggle room' needed to avoid compromising Quality while it works. Not to be confused with Sprint Objective or Forecast. *(see Sprint Objective, Sprint Forecast)*

Sprint Interrupt | At the end of the Sprint the Scrum Team interrupts the continuous flow of work and has four Ceremonies/Discussions/Meetings in order to allow for Feedback, Improvement, and Re-Planning. *(see Sprint Planning, Team Retrospective, Product Review, Progress Review)*

Sprint Objective | An objective brought to Sprint Planning by the Team Captain. The Team Captain may be accountable for the Sprint Objective – but the Team is not – and the Team is under no obligation to choose the Sprint Objective as its Sprint Goal. *(see Accountable, Sprint Goal, Sprint Planning)*

Sprint Planning | A Team session at the beginning of a Sprint in which the Team Members (including the Team Captain) discuss and negotiate amongst themselves in order to: 1) Establish Sprint End; 2) Select a Kaizen to accomplish; 3) Make sure there are enough Stories Ready or 'in progress' so the Team can get back to work; and 4) Commit to a Sprint Goal. *(see Sprint End, Kaizen, Sprint Goal)*

Sprint Retrospective | Synonym for **Team Retrospective.** *(see Team Retrospective)*

Sprint Review | The Sprint Review consists of a Product Review and a Progress Review, and may consist of other Reviews as well. These reviews often require different participants, so the Sprint Review is often a series of separate Reviews. *(see Executive Review, Project Review, Progress Review, Product Review)*

Sprint Team | The Scrum Team *along with* any external SMEs who are (either officially or unofficially) members of the Team during the Sprint.

Sprint Zero | A deprecated synonym for **Startup Sprint**. *(see Startup Sprint)*

Squad Leader | A sergeant who is in charge of a squad of soldiers and lower-ranking sergeants; often used to refer to a **Team Captain** who is also a member of the DevTeam. *(see Team Captain, DevTeam)*

Stakeholder | 1) A person with a *legitimate* interest in the Product,

Process, or Team. 2) Someone who the Scrum Team ignores 'at their peril.' 3) A person who reviews the Team's Increment at the Product Review. 4) A person who is involved with, affected by, or has an effect on, the Team. *Note: While Team Members are stakeholders, the word Stakeholder [uppercase] is usually reserved for external stakeholders.*

Standard of Care (SoC) | The Standard of Care is the part of "Done" that describes the objective criteria the Team uses to determine whether or not they used the prudence, caution, processes, and procedures that they should have when doing their work. The Standard of Care depends on the work being done; each item of work (Story, Increment, Release, etc.) could have its own Standard of Care. The Standard of Care is used to 'guarantee' sufficient technical quality to be acceptable. Failure to meet the Standard of Care is negligence, and the Team is accountable for any damages that result. The Standard of Care is often (erroneously) referred to as the Definition of Done (DoD). *(see "Done", Definition of Done)*

Startup Sprint | A specialized Sprint used to get a Team 'up and running' quickly, rather than dragging their feet *getting ready* to start development. A Startup Sprint usually includes Analysis, Team Training, Infrastructure and Environmental Work – and the development of something 'real' – and its purpose is to limit the amount of 'up front' work that takes place before actual Product is developed. It is a Sprint whose Sprint Goal is *"We will be producing real Results by the end of this Sprint"* – it is not about 'getting ready'; it is about 'getting moving'.

Stay-At-Home | In swarming, a person who 'stays with' the Story, and probably works as the Story's Coordinator. When working on Coding Stories, it is common to have a Coder as the Stay-At-Home in order to avoid context-switching. *(see Team Swarm, Coordinator)*

Story | 1) A request from a stakeholder for something of value (it could be an Epic); 2) A unit of work that is 'small enough' to be agreed to by the Team; a Backlog Item that is not an Epic. 3) (by others) A synonym for Backlog Item. 3) (by others) a synonym for User Story. *(see User Story, Backlog Item)*

Story Agreement |An agreement between the Product Owner (Team Captain) and the rest of the Team that defines when a Story will be complete (or "Done"). The Story Agreement typically consists of the Acceptance Criteria, the Standard of Care, and (possibly) additional General Agreements. This is a synonym for "Done". *(see "Done", Acceptance Criteria, Standard of Care, General Agreements)*

Story Board | A Team tool that shows the tasks that are needed in the Sprint, organized by Story. The Story Board is a 'living' document that the Team updates to reflect its current thinking; it is often updated at the Daily Scrum.

Story Owner | A Team Member (or SME) who represents the Stakeholder's interests in the Story to the rest of the Team during Planning and Development. *(see Story)*

Story Size | Synonym for **Size [of a Story].** *(see Size [of a Story])*

Story Time | Synonym for **Backlog Refinement.** *(see Backlog Refinement)*

Storyotype | A stereotype or template for a Story or Epic. Storyotypes are used to capture re-useful information common to many Stories; in particular, Storyotypes are used to capture common Standards of Care. *(see Standard of Care)*

StoryPoint | A relative measure of the size of a Story. Often confused with EffortPoint. *(see EffortPoint, Velocity, Size [of a Story])*

Strategic Agility | Agility that changes 'what' the Team or Organization does in order to maximize Value or ROI. Strategic Agility is a Product Ownership responsibility. *(compare to Tactical Agility)*

Structure | An Organization's Structure shows how the Teams, Pods, Groups, and Individuals are connected and related to each other.

STS | Acronym for **Single-Team Scrum**. *(see Single-Team Scrum)*

Subject Matter Expert (SME) | Somebody with specialized knowledge or talent that is needed by the Team; this includes SMEs on the product, the environment, development practices, and so on. The term usually refers to SMEs that are 'outside' the Team, but not always.

Sustainable Pace | The rate at which a Team can work without burning itself out. Originally called "40 Hour Week" by Kent Beck as an XP practice.

Swarm | Short for **Team Swarm**. *(see Team Swarm, Swarming)*

Swarmer | In a Team Swarm, a Swarmer is a person who is moving from Story to Story, working with those Story's Coordinators and other Swarmers, in order to offer his or her expertise and efforts wherever they are needed. *(see Team Swarm, Swarming)*

Swarming | Having several people work together on a piece of work. Common swarming patterns in software development include: *Pair Programming*, *Three-People-at-a-Whiteboard*, and *Team-at-a-Table*. *(see Team Swarm. Three-People-at-a-Whiteboard, Team-at-a-Table)*

Tactical Agility | Agility that changes 'how' a Team works in order to get to "Done"; this is embodied in the Team's Self-Organization. *(compare to Strategic Agility)*

Task | A small, undivided, 'chunk' of work to be accomplished, usually within the Team. Tasks organize the team's work plan on how they will get Stories to "Done".

Team | 1) The Scrum Team; 2) (by others) The Development Team; 3) (Ken Schwaber) A role, taken on by a group of people, that means that they are a Well-Formed Team. *(see Well-Formed Team)*

Team-at-a-Table | A Swarming Pattern used for planning, general goal-setting, and so on. As its name implies, this involves a group, sitting around a table, having open discussions. It is frequently facilitated by a Scrum Master. *(see Team Swarm)*

Team Ability | This is an Environmental Variable, and includes the capabilities of individual Team Members, the Team's frame of mind, and how well the Team synergizes. *(see Environmental Variables)*

Team Captain | The Team Member accountable for maximizing the value of the Scrum Team's Work. Each Team must have its own Team Captain to 'call the plays' about what work the Team should do next. Also commonly called the Team's Product Owner. Some Team Captains are also Squad Leaders or Crew Chiefs. *(see Product Ownership, Business Owner, Team's Product Owner, Squad Leader, Crew Chief)*

Team Facilitator | A Team Member who facilitates (makes easier) the Team's self-organization, growth, maturation, and improvement (on a daily basis) as the Team 1) does its work, 2) removes **Impediments** to progress, and 3) achieves improvement objectives, or **Kaizens**. Every Team must have a Team Facilitator, who is often a technical contributor, as well *(see Scrum Mastering, Impediment, Kaizen, Team Representative, Scrum Master)*

Team Member | Any member of the Scrum Team, including the Team Captain (Product Owner) and Team Facilitator (Scrum Master).

Team Norms | Team norms are a set of rules or guidelines that a team establishes to shape the interaction of its members with each other and with people external to the team. Team norms are used to help guide the behavior of team members and to assess how well they are behaving. *(see Conflict Resolution Process)*

Team-of-Teams | An Organization that is made up of Scrum Teams; it is often seen as a big Team whose members are Scrum Teams.

Team-Product | The Deliverable Results produced by a single Team. *(see Product, Product-Product)*

Team Representative | A Team Member who speaks for the Team; the Team Representative is normally the Team Captain. However, when Scrum Teams self-organize their Team Captain and/or Team Facilitator on an as-needed basis, we refer to a person playing this role the Team Representative. *(see Team Captain, Team Facilitator)*

Team Retrospective | A Team session at the end of a Sprint when the Team Members (facilitated by their Team Facilitator) discuss and agree upon ways they could improve their Practices, teamwork, environment, or Organization for the next Sprint.

Team Swarm | A method of working where a Team works on just a few things at a time. Each Story is finished as quickly as possible by having many people work on it together, rather than having a series of handoffs. The ultimate is Single Item Flow, where the whole Team works on one Story at a time, and finishes it completely before moving on to the next one. *(see Swarmer, Swarming, Coordinator, Stay-At-Home)*

Team Values | The Team Values are: Openness, Focus, Commitment, Respect, Courage, Visibility, Humor, and Accountability. *(see Values, Scrum Values, Kanban Values)*

Team's Product Owner | Synonym for **Team Captain.** *(see Team Captain)*

TeamLet | The Team Members and SMEs who are Swarming on a particular Story. The typical swarm involves 2-3 people at a time. *(see Team Swarm)*

Technical Debt | This is an Environmental Variable that includes deficiencies in the code, technical documentation, development environments, 3rd-party tools, and development practices, which makes it hard for the Team to modify, update, repair, or deliver the Product. *(see Environmental Variables)*

Three-People-at-a-Whiteboard | A Swarming Pattern used for problem-solving, design, and so on. As its name implies, it consists of three people, with complementary skills and knowledge, working together to solve a hard problem. This pattern is generally acknowledged to be the most powerful tool in engineering. *(see Team Swarm)*

Time-Boxed Story | Time-Boxed Stories have their Acceptance Criteria (at least partially) defined by a time-box, and the actual Results produced are limited to what can be completed (using the Story's Standard of Care) within that time-box. *(see Acceptance-Based Story, Standard of Care, "Done")*

Transformation Owner | A combination Business Owner and Scrum Master who is accountable for implementing an Agile

Transformation. The Transformation Owner is often the Team Captain of a Transformation Team. *(see Transformation Team, Business Owner, Scrum Master, Agile Transformation)*

Transformation Team | A Team that shepherds an Organization's Agile Transformation. A Transformation Team contains Agile Coaches and 'People with Power' who can 'get things done', and is (often) external to the Organization being transformed. *(see Agile Coach, Agile Transformation)*

UnDone | The phrase "UnDone work" is often used to describe the work needed to move something from "Done" to Releasable; in other words, it is work that *maybe should have been* "Done", but wasn't. Deciding what work to leave UnDone is a delicate issue. *(see "Done")*

Use Case | A Capability that represents an interaction between a User and the System in order to achieve a Goal. A Use Case consists of multiple Scenarios, and usually requires many Stories to implement, so a Use Case is usually an Epic. *(see Scenario, Epic)*

User Story | A Story whose value is for the User of the software; popularized by eXtreme Programming (XP). *(see Story)*

Validation | Validation is assuring that a Result (Capability) is fit for use; that it does what it *needs* to do. *(compare to Verification)*

Value-Driven | A Team is value-driven when the Team Members value working together; they are constantly improving themselves, their Team, their environment, and their tools; and they strive to live an appropriate set of Values. *(see Values)*

Values | The word Values, in common use, refers either to values in general, the Team Values, the Kanban Values, or the Scrum Values. *(see Team Values, Kanban Values, Scrum Values)*

Velocity | The rate that a Team or Organization *has been producing* Product; usually calculated as completed StoryPoints per Sprint. It is often used as an approximation for Capacity and is often confused with WorkRate. *(see StoryPoint, Capacity, WorkRate)*

Verification | Verification is assuring that something has met its specification; that it does as it was *intended* to do. *(compare to Validation)*

Virtual Team | A Team containing Team Members who 'live' on other Teams.

Visibility | The Team makes the current state of the Team's Product/Results visible to Stakeholders and the Business. *(see Values)*

Walking Skeleton | A subset of the System that demonstrates the basic architectural decisions; it is the result of many Architecturally Significant Stories. *(see Architecturally Significant Story)*

Well-Defined Story | A Story whose Acceptance Criteria are known. *(see Acceptance Criteria, Ready Story)*

Well-Formed Team (WFT) | A Well-Formed Team (WFT) is more than just a Team; it's a 'real Team' – a Team that knows its job, does its job, and looks good doing it. A WFT is a Team with heart and soul; where Team Members value working together to be the best Team they can be. A WFT is a team that is self-organized, self-contained, and value-driven. A Scrum Team is a well-formed team that has both a Product Owner and a Scrum Master, and it is a primary teaching of Scrum that all teams (especially those working in complex domains) should be well-formed. *(see Self-Organized, Self-Contained, Value-Driven)*

Whole Team | The Scrum Team along with its Subject Matter Experts and its Stakeholders; this is the 'whole team' involved in production.

WIBNI (wib'·nee) **|** stands for **W**ouldn't **I**t **B**e **N**ice If, and represents things that we wish were true, but aren't – so we must *get over* them; example is *"wouldn't it be nice if we had more testers…"*

WIP | Acronym for **Work in Progress.** *(see Work in Progress)*

WIP Limit | The maximum number of Stories allowed in the Work in Progress at any given time. *(see Work in Progress)*

Work Backlog | The Team's Work Backlog is owned by the Team Captain and consists of Stories that are being refined to become Ready for Planning. These Stories are of two types: Capabilities and Chores. The Capabilities in the Work Backlog can be referred to as the Team-Product's Product Backlog. *(see Product Backlog, Ready Story, Capability, Chore, Team-Product)*

Work in Progress (WIP) | The Stories that the Team is currently working on. *(see Backlog)*

Work Item | The Work Items the Scrum Team works on are called Stories, and as the Team completes the Stories, they produce Results in an iterative and incremental manner, thus providing opportunities for meaningful feedback from Stakeholders.

WFT | Acronym for **Well-Formed Team.** *(see Well-Formed Team)*

Workgroup | Synonym for **Cross-Cutting Workgroup**. *(see Cross-Cutting Workgroup)*

WorkRate | The rate that a Team expends effort; usually calculated as EffortPoints per Sprint, Ideal Engineering Hours/Days per Sprint, or something similar. It is used as an aid in Sprint Planning, and is often confused with Velocity. *(see EffortPoints, Ideal Engineering Hours/Days, Velocity)*

Work Results | Whatever the Team produces; consists of the Increment (partial and potential deliverables) and non-deliverables, such as Chores. *(see Increment, Chore)*

XP | Acronym for **eXtreme Programming.** *(see eXtreme Programming)*

Zombie Scrum | Any of the Scrums that the *Scrum Guide* replaced; they don't have a Team Captain and/or they commit to completing their Sprint Backlogs. *(see Scrum Guide, Sprint Backlog, Team's Product Owner)*

Nine Zones of Scrum

There are two major discriminators when looking at types of Scrum: the Product Ownership, and Sprint Planning. There are three types of each, leading to Nine Zones of Scrum, as we see in the picture.

	Locked-Down Sprint	Adaptable Sprint	Continuous Planning
(both) Team's & Product's Product Owners	Scrum 2.5	Scrum 2.75	Scrum 3.0
(only) Team's Product Owner	Scrum 1.75	Scrum 2.0	Scrum 2.25
(only) Product's Product Owner	Scrum 1.0	Scrum 1.25	Scrum 1.5

The Scrums that are 'grayed-out' are the 'zombie' Scrums (Scrums that the Scrum Guide tried to kill, but won't stay dead), while the four Scrums in the upper-right corner are the 'modern' Scrums (Scrums that comply with the Scrum Guide).

The Agile Manifesto

Manifesto for Agile Software Development

We are uncovering better ways of developing software by doing it and helping others do it. Through this work we have come to value:

Individuals and interactions over processes and tools
Working software over comprehensive documentation
Customer collaboration over contract negotiation
Responding to change over following a plan

That is, while there is value in the items on the right, we value the items on the left more.

Kent Beck	James Grenning	Robert C. Martin
Mike Beedle	Jim Highsmith	Steve Mellor
Arie van Bennekum	Andrew Hunt	Ken Schwaber
Alistair Cockburn	Ron Jeffries	Jeff Sutherland
Ward Cunningham	Jon Kern	Dave Thomas
Martin Fowler	Brian Marick	

Twelve Principles of Agile Software

Our highest priority is to satisfy the customer through early and continuous delivery of valuable software.

Welcome changing requirements, even late in development. Agile processes harness change for the customer's competitive advantage.

Deliver working software frequently, from a couple of weeks to a couple of months, with a preference to the shorter timescale.

Business people and developers must work together daily throughout the project.

Build projects around motivated individuals. Give them the environment and support they need, and trust them to get the job done.

The most efficient and effective method of conveying information to and within a development team is face-to-face conversation.

Working software is the primary measure of progress.

Agile processes promote sustainable development. The sponsors, developers, and users should be able to maintain a constant pace indefinitely.

Continuous attention to technical excellence and good design enhances agility.

Simplicity--the art of maximizing the amount of work not done--is essential.

The best architectures, requirements, and designs emerge from self-organizing teams.

At regular intervals, the team reflects on how to become more effective, then tunes and adjusts its behavior accordingly.

Single-Team Scrum (STS)

At its core, Scrum is a model showing how a single Team produces Results for Stakeholders. The $Scrum_H$ model of single-Team Scrum is a clean, flexible, description of Scrum that is appropriate for most Organizations...

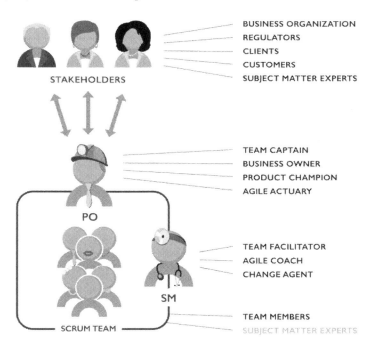

For more, read our book: *Scrum Handbook: Single-Team Scrum*

Multi-Team Scrum (MTS)

Single-Team Scrum is about a single Scrum Team producing results in an incremental, iterative, and agile way, in order to maximize the value it can provide for its Stakeholders... even though the Stakeholders are changing their minds, and disagreeing with each other, about what they want. Many people (in Organizations bigger than a single team) have seen this happen, and have asked: "How can I use Scrum to increase my Organization's capacity to provide value?"

We call this the **Scaling Problem**.

Now, Scaling, in general, is defined as "an Organization's response to a need to change capacity," which can either be an increase (scaling up) or a decrease (scaling down). In this Handbook we will be discussing primarily 'scaling up' or, simply, scaling. Even though capacity can be improved with better techniques and tools, we will consider that to be 'continuous improvement' and not scaling.

We will view Organizations as "Teams-of-Teams," and the Organization's shape is crucial because it determines the primary pieces of the Organization and the lines of communication between them.

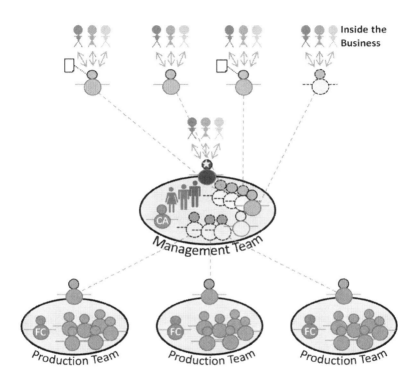

For more, read our book: *Scrum Handbook: Multi-Team Scrum*

Acknowledgements

We have both been involved with Scrum for over 20 years, and we'd like to thank Ken Schwaber and Jeff Sutherland for bringing Scrum to the software community. Without them, there would be no Scrum.

We would also like to thank all the teams we have worked with and observed, and all our students who have brought us news and information about their Scrum teams. We know that *"Scrum is what successful Scrum Teams do,"* and without this feedback about what successful Scrum Teams do, there would also be no Scrum.

Good luck, and happy scrumming!

About the Authors

Dan Rawsthorne

Dan has developed software in an agile way since 1983. He has worked in many different domains, from e-commerce to military avionics. He has a PhD in Mathematics (number theory), is a retired Army Officer, and is a Professional Bowler and Coach. Dan is very active in the Agile/Scrum community and speaks at conferences and seminars. He is a transformation agent, helping Organizations become more successful through agility. His non-software background helps him immeasurably: his mathematics back-ground tells him to look for underlying problems rather than focus on symptoms; his military career gave him experience in teamwork and empowerment; and his work with bowlers helps him understand that coaching is a two-way street.

Doug Shimp

Doug has worked in the technology field since 1992 and has played many key roles on software teams, including Coder, Tester, Analyst, Team Leader, Manager, Coach, and Consultant. Doug's passion is for team learning to improve product development, and he is a leader in the area of Agile/Scrum transitions and applied practices. He believes that the core basis for applied agility is that 'You must see the result for it to be real; otherwise it is all just theory...' Much of his experience with teamwork and agility comes from outside the software field, including an earlier career as an owner/manager of a painting company – which enables him to learn about small-team dynamics in a very hands-on way.

For More Information

To learn more about 3Back, LLC and our Scrum-related services contact us at info@3back.com. Follow @Scrum_Coach on Twitter, and to subscribe to our newsletter, visit: https://3back.com/blog/.

We Make Teams Better

We don't just talk Agile, we live Agile. Our 3Back Team is a well-formed, Agile team; applying Scrum$_H$ in our own workplace. From our hands-on support staff to our seasoned consultants and trainers, every member of the 3Back Team is, at a minimum, a CSM (Certified Scrum Master). Within every level of the 3Back Team, we bring a real-world appreciation and understanding of your team's needs.

For Help With Your Company's Scrum: info@3Back.com

For Training: training@3Back.com

Managing Work

At 3Back we are a fully distributed team. We actively build and manage Get To Done (gettodone.com), an online Scrum software development tool. Get To Done helps us train as a pedagogical tool, explore new ways of collaborating and focus our most precious resource – attention – on work being done.

Made in the USA
Columbia, SC
30 April 2022